SUPER SKILLS

HOW TO
CODE 2.0

Pushing Your Skills Further

with **PYTHON**

ELIZABETH TWEEDALE

Walter Foster
Jr.

Quarto is the authority on a wide range of topics.
Quarto educates, entertains and enriches the lives of our readers—
enthusiasts and lovers of hands-on living.
www.quartoknows.com

First published in the UK by
QED Publishing
A Quarto Group Company
The Old Brewery
6 Blundell Street
London N7 9BH

Publisher: Maxime Boucknooghe
Editorial Director: Laura Knowles
Art Director: Susi Martin
Project Editor: Carly Madden
Editor: Diyan Leake
Design: Kevin Knight
Original Illustrations: Venetia Dean
Consultant: Sean M. Tracey

ABOUT THE AUTHOR

Elizabeth Tweedale is the founder of Cypher,
a company dedicated to teaching computer
science in new and exciting ways to children
during vacation camps. She is the co-author
of the *Kids Get Coding* series (Wayland, 2016),
a computer scientist, and a consultant to leading
architectural offices worldwide, advising them how
to incorporate code into their design processes.

6 Orchard Road, Suite 100
Lake Forest, CA 92630
quartoknows.com
Visit our blogs at quartoknows.com

Printed in China

1 3 5 7 9 10 8 6 4 2

MIX
Paper from
responsible sources
FSC® C016973

CONTENTS

WELCOME TO THE WORLD OF CODING

Anyone can code! That's right—all you need to become a great coder are creativity and curiosity. Code is behind nearly everything in the world these days. So, once you learn how to code, you can change the world and become anything you want to be!

More and more jobs in the future will require code. This book is broken down into ten super skills, each one based on a different job. We're going to learn how the programming language Python can help us with these skills.

CAN I LEARN TO CODE?

Yes, of course! No previous coding knowledge is required to learn to code using this book. However, if you've already tried simpler programming languages such as Scratch, it will be much easier to learn to code in Python. The biggest difference with Python is that it's a text-based language—you'll have to type out your instructions using the keyboard, unlike Scratch, where you write programs using blocks that snap together.

HOW THIS BOOK IS ORGANIZED

This book will introduce you to ten core skills for coding. We'll be using the programming language Python to explore how code is used in different job industries out in the real world. It is best to read the chapters in the right order, because each chapter introduces new ideas that build on the previous chapter. If you skip a chapter, you might miss something important.

HANDY TIP!

If you haven't done any coding, try learning Scratch with *Super Skills: How to Code in 10 Easy Lessons* first!

WHAT IS CODE?

Code is found inside the technology that we use every day. It is the set of instructions given to a computer in order for it to know what to do. Knowing how to give those instructions to different kinds of technology, from our mobile phones to software that counts election votes, is what coding is all about. You might not realize it, but learning to code will help you become more of an expert in any job you choose in the future.

Coding a program is just like writing a book. Each set of instructions is like a sentence, and we have to write many sentences in a row to write a book. A "book" in coding is called a program, which is the set of instructions that tell the whole story about what we're telling technology to do for us.

WE WILL EXPLORE MORE JOBS THAT USE CODE AS WE GAIN MORE SUPER SKILLS THROUGHOUT THE BOOK!

Code is what makes the gadgets in your life work. For example, a mobile phone would just be a fancy piece of metal with lights if it weren't for the code telling it how to connect calls, or instruct the apps that you use. But did you know code can be linked to all kinds of different industries and jobs throughout the world?

AIRLINE PILOT: Code is used for the autopilot program that the pilot can use to have the airplane fly on its own.

MEDICAL SCIENTIST: Code is used in programs that can help predict when people will get sick by looking at lots of data from sick people.

FARMER: Code is even used in farming! Tiny sensors used in grain bins help monitor the correct temperature, and GPS satellites can track the whole crop from 12,400 miles (20,000 km) above the earth.

CODE IN YOUR LIFE

Think about the jobs your family and friends do. How do they use technology? Can you think of ways that using code would help them in their jobs? How would code help you at school? Could it help with homework?

CODING IN THE WORLD

We can use different programming languages to do the same task, but different programming languages are good at different things. So how do we choose which one to use?

CHOOSING A LANGUAGE

Thinking about the different kinds of tasks we'd like to do, and knowing what languages are good at what, can help us choose which language to use. Since most programming languages cover the majority of coding concepts, let's choose a language somewhere in the middle.

A good learning progression might look something like this.

SCRATCH JR: A visual programming language that uses blocks and pictures to introduce coding.

SCRATCH: More visual fun with text blocks that are used to create games and animations.

PYTHON: Text-based programming language that is easy to use and good at different tasks.

HTML/CSS/JAVASCRIPT: The three main languages used on most websites.

C++/JAVA: Advanced programming languages that are used to write fast-running programs.

IF YOU ONLY EVER LEARN ONE LANGUAGE, YOU SHOULD BE ABLE TO SOLVE MOST CODING PROBLEMS—SOME WILL JUST BE EASIER THAN OTHERS. IMAGINE TRYING TO COMMUNICATE WITH SOMEONE WHO DOESN'T SPEAK YOUR LANGUAGE. YOU CAN DO IT. IT'S JUST A BIT TRICKIER!

TECHNOLOGY IS CHANGING THE WORLD

So, in what way exactly is technology changing the world? We can break it down into seven main areas, which we call mega trends!

1 PEOPLE AND THE INTERNET

People can interact with objects that are linked to the internet, such as the clothes they wear or the buildings they live in.

2 SUPERCOMPUTERS

Computers are getting smaller and cheaper, making it easier for everyone to have a fast and useful computer. Compared to a computer from 15 years ago, a smartphone is a supercomputer!

3 THE INTERNET OF THINGS

Tiny sensors are being added to all sorts of computers and devices to help us keep track of all the data out there, such as weather patterns in Antarctica and how much the ice is melting in the Arctic!

4 BIG DATA

Tiny sensors connected to the internet collect huge amounts of data. Problem-solving programs can learn from this data and help us resolve issues and answer big questions.

5 ARTIFICIAL INTELLIGENCE

When problem-solving programs look at big data and start forming new questions, we call this artificial intelligence. Not only can these programs learn from what they find, but they also have the ability to write their own code and evolve.

6 SHARING IS CARING!

The internet makes it easier for people to share information. You can easily use the computer to talk about your science homework to someone who lives on the other side of the world!

7 3D PRINTING

Physical objects can now be printed in 3D. If you need a screwdriver at home but can't find one—well, you can just 3D-print a new one!

WHAT DO I NEED?

A computer is required to learn Python; a desktop or laptop will do. You'll also need internet access in order to download the software you will need.

DIVE IN!

In this book, you are learning key Computer Science concepts. Computer Science is the study of computers and technology—a tricky subject! Don't worry if you find some of the examples too complicated. By trying out more advanced concepts, even without fully comprehending all of the details, you will get a better understanding of the "why?" of coding. This will motivate you to learn more about coding in the future.

The examples in this book use Python 3.5.2 and some of its new features. If you're using an older version of Python, such as 2.7, some of the examples might not work.

ASK FOR HELP!

If you get stuck, try asking Google for help. You can always copy and paste error messages (from bugs you have in your code) into the Google search page, which will usually send you to a helpful answer. Another website with good answers and people who can help with your questions is www.stackoverflow.com, a popular site for asking coding-related questions about any text-based language.

REMEMBER TO ALWAYS ASK AN ADULT BEFORE GOING ONLINE!

HANDY TIP!
If you get stuck, all of the code from this book can be found on the How To Code 2.0 Repository on **GitHub**. https://github. com/elizabethtweedale/ HowToCode2

HANDY TIP!
It's always a good idea to update your computer to the latest operating system before downloading new software.

LET'S GET TYPING, QWERTY!

Since you're going to be typing away at your Python code, it's important to first learn some basic touch-typing skills. Follow these easy steps to get started and then go online to practice!

SIT UP STRAIGHT

- Sit up, keeping your back straight.
- Bend your elbows.
- Keep a distance of at least 18–28 inches (45–70 cm) between your eyes and the screen. You can think of this distance as about two or three basketballs put together.

HOME ROW—FIND THE BUMPS

- The home row is the row of keys that your fingers rest on when they are not typing.
- The F and J keys have raised bumps on them, indicating where you should put your index fingers. The bumps are also handy for finding the keys without looking. Give it a try!
- Rest your fingers on the A, S, D, F and J, K, L, and ; (semicolon) keys. These eight keys are the home row.
- Place your wrists on the space in front of the keyboard.

KEYS + FINGERS

Each key has a specific finger assigned to it. See if you can work out which fingers you need to use to reach the other letters on the keyboard.

FINGER MOTION

- Make sure to only move the finger used to press the needed key.
- When you finish pressing the key you need, return your finger to the home row.
- Did you know the keyboard was designed with your hands in mind? The keys are arranged in such a way to make it easier to move your fingers around to all of the letter keys with as little movement as possible.

THE KEYBOARD IS SOMETIMES CALLED A QWERTY KEYBOARD. THIS IS BECAUSE THE FIRST SIX KEYS ON THE TOP LEFT LETTER ROW SPELL QWERTY.

SPEED

Take your time. It is more important to be accurate than to be speedy at the beginning.

PRACTICE MAKES PERFECT!

The best way to get comfortable with typing is to practice. Test it out at one of these free online sites:

www.ratatype.com
www.typingclub.com

HANDY TIP!
Don't peek! Cover your hands with a light cloth so that you are sure to not look at your keyboard as you type.

INSTALLING PYTHON

Python is easy to learn because the code can be read by a human fairly easily, and the Python **Interpreter** can pick up on any bugs in your code. It is forgiving when it comes to the number of spaces or tabs you need in your code, and doesn't have as many special characters as C++ and Java. With Python, it's easy to write complex programs with just a few lines of code.

LET'S INTERPRET!

Interpreters are people who know two languages. The program we will be downloading and installing in order to write our code in the Python programming language is called the Python Interpreter. Its job is to translate what we are telling it via Python, into a language that the tiny bits and bytes of the computer can understand!

HANDY TIP!

Python is an **open source software**, meaning you can download and install it with a simple internet connection! Open source software is software with source code that anyone can inspect, modify, and enhance. (http://www.opensource.org) The opposite is proprietary software, such as Microsoft Office or Adobe Creative Cloud, which you have to pay for.

THE LANGUAGES THAT THE BITS AND BYTES OF THE COMPUTER UNDERSTAND ARE WHAT'S CALLED "LOW LEVEL" PROGRAMMING LANGUAGES.

1 GO TO

Open a web browser and go to www.python.org

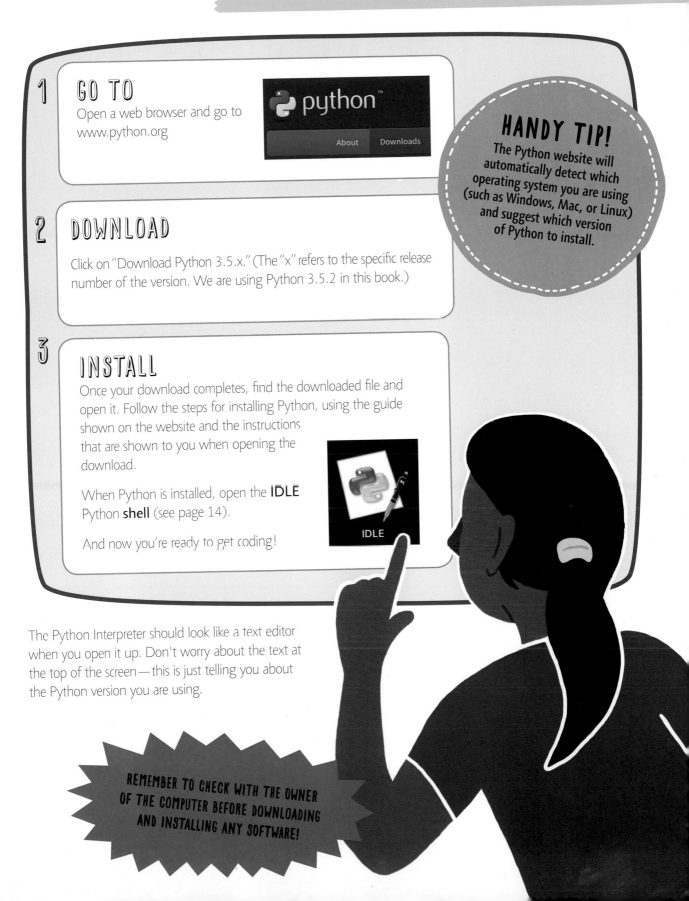

HANDY TIP!
The Python website will automatically detect which operating system you are using (such as Windows, Mac, or Linux) and suggest which version of Python to install.

2 DOWNLOAD

Click on "Download Python 3.5.x." (The "x" refers to the specific release number of the version. We are using Python 3.5.2 in this book.)

3 INSTALL

Once your download completes, find the downloaded file and open it. Follow the steps for installing Python, using the guide shown on the website and the instructions that are shown to you when opening the download.

When Python is installed, open the **IDLE** Python **shell** (see page 14).

And now you're ready to get coding!

The Python Interpreter should look like a text editor when you open it up. Don't worry about the text at the top of the screen—this is just telling you about the Python version you are using.

REMEMBER TO CHECK WITH THE OWNER OF THE COMPUTER BEFORE DOWNLOADING AND INSTALLING ANY SOFTWARE!

BECOME A PROGRAMMER

To become a programmer, you have to first learn how to write a program using code. For this skill, you will learn how to communicate with the computer using Python and then create, save, and run your first program.

WHAT DOES A PROGRAMMER DO?

A programmer writes programs for computers to follow. Programmers come from many different backgrounds with lots of different interests. They write the code for different types of programs, from web applications like Facebook (Mark Zuckerberg) to programming languages like Python (Guido van Rossum). Programmers can work on their own, but more and more work together as part of a team.

HOW DOES THE COMPUTER FOLLOW A PROGRAM?

As a programmer, your job is to communicate with the hardware of the computer. You tell it how to analyze data and solve the problems that you give it.

The code you write is given to the central processing unit (**CPU**) to process. The CPU is like the command center of the computer. It communicates your instructions to and from the **input** and **output** devices, the memory, and the networks.

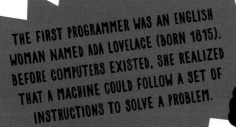

THE FIRST PROGRAMMER WAS AN ENGLISH WOMAN NAMED ADA LOVELACE (BORN 1815). BEFORE COMPUTERS EXISTED, SHE REALIZED THAT A MACHINE COULD FOLLOW A SET OF INSTRUCTIONS TO SOLVE A PROBLEM.

INPUTS AND OUTPUTS

○ Input and output devices are what we use to communicate with the computer. These include the keyboard, screen, mouse, touchpad, printer, scanner, speaker, and microphone.

○ A network is the connection from your computer to other computers. The most common network we use is the internet!

○ The CPU uses the computer's memory to store information it uses to run its programs. Memory can also be stored in external devices such as USBs or flash drives.

HARDWARE

CPU   RAM memory

INPUTS & OUTPUTS

speakers

mouse

printer

NETWORK

internet

MEMORY & STORAGE   flash drive

back-up drive

HANDY TIP!
In this book we will use the term "program," although most of our code will be simple and could be called scripts.

TAKE IT FURTHER

CAN YOU DETERMINE WHICH OF THE ITEMS SHOWN ABOVE ARE INPUT DEVICES TO THE COMPUTER AND WHICH ARE OUTPUT DEVICES FROM IT?

YOUR FIRST PROGRAM

To type in and run your programs, you'll use the program's **shell**. The Python shell is called **IDLE**, which stands for Interactive Development Environment. IDLE makes it easier to write Python programs, the same way word-processing software such as Word or Pages makes it easier to write books.

THE IDLE SHELL

Now that you have mastered Super Skill 1 by downloading Python, you will find a few new programs on your computer. Find the IDLE shell and open it. You should see a window like this:

```
_ □ X
Python 3.5.2 (v3.5.2:4def2a2901a5, Jun 26 2016, 10:47:25)
[GCC 4.2.1 (Apple Inc. build 5666) (dot 3)] on darwin
Type "copyright", "credits" or "license()" for more information.
>>>
```

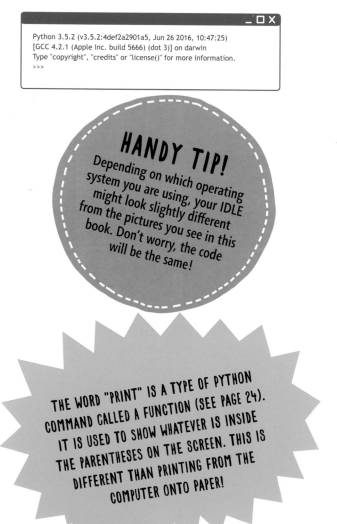

HANDY TIP!
Depending on which operating system you are using, your IDLE might look slightly different from the pictures you see in this book. Don't worry, the code will be the same!

THE WORD "PRINT" IS A TYPE OF PYTHON COMMAND CALLED A FUNCTION (SEE PAGE 24). IT IS USED TO SHOW WHATEVER IS INSIDE THE PARENTHESES ON THE SCREEN. THIS IS DIFFERENT THAN PRINTING FROM THE COMPUTER ONTO PAPER!

LET'S TALK

Once you have opened the Python shell, you should see this:

```
● ● ●
>>>
```

This prompt is Python's way of telling you it's ready for you to give it an instruction. All you have to know is how to speak the Python language!

Let's give it a try. Type:

```
● ● ●
>>> print ("Hello World")
```

At the end of the line, press Return (or Enter). If you've entered the code correctly, you will notice that the Python shell says:

```
● ● ●
Hello World
```

Well done! You have written a tiny program and had your first conversation with Python! Now, let's check for errors and then save the conversation so that we can have it over and over again.

THE FIRST PROGRAM

"Hello World" is a well-known first program for coders. It's like the programmer saying hello to the computer and the computer saying hello back. In reality, you have simply given the computer an instruction to display the words "Hello World."

AAARGH!

SYNTAX ERROR

Syntax is the group of rules of a programming language. These rules are very important in order for the computer to know what you are trying to tell it using a language that it can understand.

Imagine trying to say **"Coding is the coolest thing in the world"** to someone but you really said: **"World thing is in the coding coolest the."** It wouldn't make very much sense to them because the second phrase doesn't follow the syntax, or rules of the English language. This is the same for Python. Let's have a look at an example.

Try typing what's below, deliberately leaving out the second quotation mark (") from your previous program:

```
print ("Hello World)
```

You will receive the following:

```
SyntaxError: EOL while scanning string literal
```

These error messages are useful to catch any mistakes we've made.

MOST COMMON SYNTAX ERRORS AND HOW TO FIX THEM

1 "unexpected indent" – Check that the extra spaces at the beginning of the lines match what is expected. The spaces are the indentation.

2 "EOL while scanning string literal" – Check that you're not missing quotation marks from the beginning and end of your lines (strings).

3 "invalid syntax" – Check for spelling mistakes.

4 "invalid syntax" – Check that you've used the correct quotation marks (" or ')

5 "invalid syntax" – Check that you haven't confused a dash (-) with an underscore (_)

6 "invalid syntax" – Check that you're using the correct brackets. The most common brackets in Python are (and) but the other two types are sometimes used as well: [ ] and { }.

SAVE THE CONVERSATION

The program you just wrote is great, but imagine if it were a conversation that you had to have with the computer every day. It would be much easier to save the conversation (or program, in this case) instead of having to rewrite it each time! Saving Python programs will become very useful when we have longer and more complicated programs to write later on.

° In the IDLE shell, click on File › New File.

° This will create an empty document which looks like a text editor. The only difference is that when using the text editor from the Python IDLE, it highlights important words using different colors and also gives tips and hints while typing, known as **autocompletion**.

° Type the following into your Untitled window:

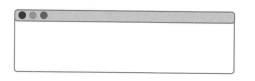

> >>> **print ("Hello World")**

COLORS

Colors are used to help you differentiate between different types of words. Did you notice the three different colors for **>>>**, the **"Hello World"** you typed and the **"Hello World"** Python returned back to you?

> >>>

> "Hello World"

> Hello World

PYTHON SCRIPT FILES HAVE NAMES THAT END WITH .PY

° Choose File › Save.

° Save your file as HelloWorld.py on your desktop.

° Choose Run › Run module.

° You should see your program run in the IDLE shell. If you close the IDLE window and run your program again, the IDLE shell will reappear and your program will run again.

Congratulations, you have just created, saved, and ran your first program!

GET COMFORTABLE

It is easiest to run programs using IDLE, but we can also use the Python launcher to open Python files through the **Terminal**. The "Terminal" (on Mac or Linux) or "Command Prompt" (on Windows) is an application on your computer where you can send commands directly to the operating system of the computer.

- Find the HelloWorld.py file you just created.
- Right-click on the file and choose Open with, and then select Python launcher. This will open up your Terminal or Command Prompt and run the Python code.
- You can also try simply double-clicking on the file!
- Look at the terminal and see if you can find where it has written "Hello world."

CALCULATOR

Python is written to understand mathematical operations such as addition (+), subtraction (-), multiplication (*), and division (/). The symbols used by Python to perform these operations are called **operators**. With these operators, we can use Python as a calculator.

Open IDLE and type the following commands:

```
5 + 5
20 – 10
9 * 3
18 / 2
```

Well done—you've turned Python into your very own calculator! You can now type and send interpreted code to the computer, write and save a program, and understand what the colors and error messages mean in your code using Super Skill 2. Now you've got the basic skills to be a programmer!

HANDY TIP!

Try pressing F5 to run your program. Shortcuts are a good way to speed up your coding. If you take a look in the menu options, you will see shortcuts next to File > New, File > Save, and many of the other commands as well.

$$\frac{\left(\left(\left(3+5\right)^2+8\right)+3\right)+5^2}{\sqrt{10}\left(1^2+2^2+3^2+4^2\right)}=?$$

TAKE IT FURTHER

TRY MORE COMPLEX EQUATIONS USING MULTIPLE OPERATORS AND PARENTHESES LIKE THIS:
((6 + 2) * 10) / 4

BECOME AN ARTIST

Artists create works of art using many different types of tools. We usually think of things like paintbrushes, pencils, sculpting tools, or cameras, but modern-day artists are also using code to create their art. For this super skill, you will learn how to use Python **modules** to create works of art using code.

WHAT IS A DIGITAL ARTIST?

A digital artist uses technology to create art. This can be anything from editing photos using scripts to writing code that creates patterns. Some exciting art installations even react to the audience by creating art as people walk by. This is done using sensors to detect where people are and code to draw specific things when the sensors detect movement.

For your first drawing as a digital artist, you are going to use code to create a drawing on the computer screen. How will you do this? Let's take a close look at the screen your drawing will be on.

Screens are made up of **pixels**. The pixels are so tiny and close together we cannot see them individually on the screen. But if we zoom in, we can see they are arranged like a grid of small squares. Each pixel can be turned on and off, like a tiny light, in any color we choose. All we have to do is tell the computer which pixels to light up, and in which colors on the screen!

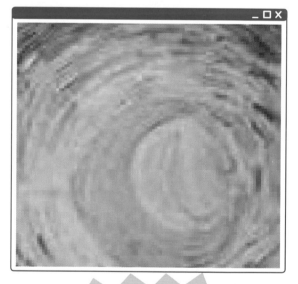

TAKE IT FURTHER

YOU CAN CREATE A PICTURE USING PIXELS! USING A PENCIL, FILL IN SQUARES ON A PIECE OF GRID PAPER TO CREATE YOUR DRAWING. TRY USING DIFFERENT COLOURED PENCILS FOR AN EXTRA CHALLENGE.

THE DESIGN OF REALLY OLD VIDEO GAMES LIKE LEGEND OF ZELDA AND SUPER MARIO WAS BASED ON LIGHTING UP PIXELS.

DRAWING WITH CODE

Python comes with a standard library of built-in modules. A module is a small chunk of code that performs a function. Think of it as a library of books, where each book is a module. If you want to use one of the books, all you have to do is look it up instead of writing it again yourself. In the same way, we can import a module to help us with our drawing.

THE TURTLE MODULE

The Turtle module has a history in coding dating back to the 1960s. It was first used as part of a programming language called Logo. It is made up of **functions** (or instructions) for creating simple drawings on the screen such as lines, dots, and curves. Think of these functions as chapters within a book. Each function has the code needed to do different tasks, such as drawing a line or filling in a circle with color.

EXAMPLES TO LEARN FROM

Before you see this module in action with your own code, let's first look at the examples that Python's Turtle module comes with. Open your Terminal (if you are using Mac or Linux) or your Command Prompt (if you are using Windows) and type in:

```
python3 -m turtledemo
```

Choose an example from the menu and press Start.

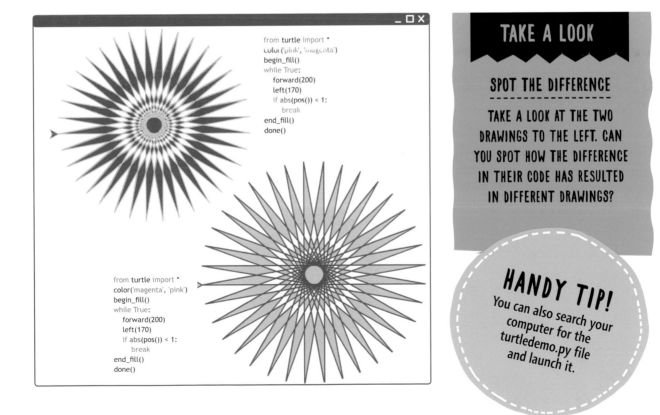

```
from turtle import *
color('pink', 'magenta')
begin_fill()
while True:
    forward(200)
    left(170)
    if abs(pos()) < 1:
        break
end_fill()
done()
```

```
from turtle import *
color('magenta', 'pink')
begin_fill()
while True:
    forward(200)
    left(170)
    if abs(pos()) < 1:
        break
end_fill()
done()
```

TAKE A LOOK

SPOT THE DIFFERENCE

TAKE A LOOK AT THE TWO DRAWINGS TO THE LEFT. CAN YOU SPOT HOW THE DIFFERENCE IN THEIR CODE HAS RESULTED IN DIFFERENT DRAWINGS?

HANDY TIP!

You can also search your computer for the turtledemo.py file and launch it.

TURTLE SQUARE

So let's get drawing! The easiest way to understand the Turtle module is to imagine a robotic turtle inside the module that knows how to draw and follows your instructions. It knows different commands such as: move forward, turn right, and turn left. By combining these instructions, you can easily get your robot turtle to create intricate shapes and pictures with just a few lines of code!

Open the **IDLE shell**. Type:

```
import turtle
>>> t = turtle.Turtle( )

#this line of code has named the turtle "t".
```

It opens the Python Turtle graphics window and shows you your Turtle (which looks like an arrow).

```
>>> t.forward(50)
#this moves the turtle forward 50 pixels.
```

Now type these lines:

```
>>> t.right(90)
>>> t.forward(50)
>>> t.right(90)
>>> t.forward(50)
>>> t.right(90)
>>> t.forward(50)
```

Well done! You've just used code to draw a square.

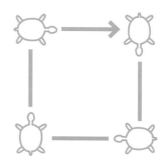
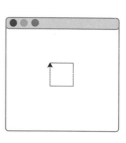

How the turtle moves   The output square from your code

HASHTAG COMMENTS

The # sign is used for commenting. Python's **Interpreter** will ignore anything after the # sign. Comments are notes that you write in the code for yourself or other programmers to read. Good programmers comment quite a lot in their code to make it quicker to read through! Comments will actually appear in red on your screen.

SAVE YOUR SQUARE

You can now copy and paste this code into a new file to save it for later.

∘ Choose File > New.
∘ Copy the code from your IDLE screen by selecting it all and choosing Edit > Copy.
∘ In your new file, choose Edit > Paste.
∘ Choose File > Save and save your file as: simpleSquare.py.
∘ Test the program you just saved by choosing Run > Run module.

IMPORTING A MODULE WILL TELL PYTHON THAT YOU WANT TO USE IT.

THE LOOPY TURTLE!

You will notice that the last code we wrote has the same two lines of code, repeated three times. One of the best parts of coding is getting the computer to repeat simple steps for you, over and over. This is called **iteration**. Repeating identical or similar steps over and over again without making errors is something that computers are very good at, and something humans sometimes struggle with. To test this, try drawing six squares on a piece of paper, all the exact same size, one next to another, and all the same distance apart from each other…tricky!

Python gives us different loop instructions to choose from, such as a **"for" loop** for repeating code a certain number of times or a **"while" loop** for repeating code until something else happens.

COLONS AND TABS

- At the end of the first line of each loop instruction, you must always include a colon (:).
- All of the code that is inside the loop will start with four spaces. These are added automatically when you type in IDLE, but you can also add them in yourself if you need to.
- When the code you want to loop is finished, your next line of code should not start with spaces, it should return to the left margin.

"FOR" LOOP

Let's create the same square we just did using a "for" loop. This time you can name your turtle something different. We call ours "loopy."

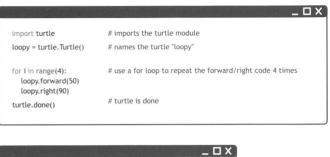

```
import turtle              # imports the turtle module
loopy = turtle.Turtle()    # names the turtle "loopy"

for i in range(4):         # use a for loop to repeat the forward/right code 4 times
    loopy.forward(50)
    loopy.right(90)
turtle.done()              # turtle is done
```

Here is the "for" loop. Type in as follows:

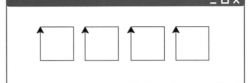

```
for i in range(4):
    loopy.forward(50)
    loopy.right(90)
```

for and **in** tell Python we are using a "for" loop.

A VARIABLE IS SOMETHING THAT CAN CHANGE, SUCH AS WEATHER (BECAUSE IT CAN BE SUNNY, RAINY, CLOUDY…).

i is the iterator. The **i** is a **variable** (see page 34) and you can name it (almost) anything you choose. It keeps track of the number of times the loop has run. It starts with 0 and then increases by 1 each time the code loops until it is 4, in this case, and then it stops the loop.

range is a **function**, like **print**, and it tells Python the number of times to repeat the loop.

MAKE A SPIROGRAPH

Artists use spirographs to make beautiful patterns. A spirograph is a tool that has interlocking wheels with holes in them for a pen to pass through to make a pattern. Let's try making a spirograph picture using code. To do this, we will use another kind of loop called the "while" loop.

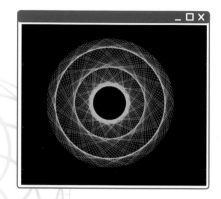

"WHILE" LOOP

Unlike the "for" loop, which repeats a specific number of times, the "while" loop will keep repeating until something changes. It is sometimes known as an infinite loop, meaning unless we tell it, it could continue for ever! For example, imagine we said:

While there is air, breathe.

This would be helpful, as we would keep breathing. But what if we said:

While there is air, laugh.

This would make you laugh forever! But what about this:

While you are being tickled, laugh.

Whew! Now you can stop laughing when we stop tickling you. OK, now that we're done laughing, let's try out a "while" loop to make a spirograph picture.

```
from turtle import *        # imports the turtle module
                            # * stands for all, which makes things easier

speed(0)                    # sets the speed of drawing to 0, which is the fastest
pencolor('pink')            # sets the color of the pen/lines to pink
bgcolor('black')            # sets the color of the background/canvas to black

x = 0                       # creates a variable x with value 0

                            # move turtle over
penup()                     # pick up the pen
lt(180)                     # lt() means rotate left by a certain angle
fd(100)                     # fd() means move forward, bk() means move back
rt(90)                      # rt() means rotate right
pendown()                   # place the pen back down for drawing

while x < 120:              # while the value of x is less than 120, continue
    fd(150)
    rt(62)
    fd(150)
    rt(62)
    fd(150)
    rt(62)
    fd(150)
    rt(62)
    fd(150)
    rt(62)
    fd(150)
    rt(62)

    rt(12.25)
    x = x+1                 # adds 1 to the value of x

exitonclick()              # when you click, turtle exits
```

HANDY TIP!

Notice the rt(90) in the code. The 90 is telling the turtle to turn 90 degrees and the rt is telling the turtle to turn toward the right. Degrees measure the angle to turn from 0 to 360. Turning around in a complete circle is 360 degrees.

RANDOM!

When something is **random**, it is in an unexpected order. For example, if you list the days of the week as they happen, they are not in a random order. However, if you choose each day of the week out of a hat and place them in order that way, they would be considered to be in a random order.

Digital artists use "random" to create unique artwork. To make things more interesting for your spirograph artwork, you can use another module that Python comes with— the Random module! This module contains useful functions for choosing or shuffling numbers at random. We will use one function (randint) to choose random numbers in order to create different colors of lines.

RGB

RGB stands for red, green, blue. Colors on your screen can be defined by mixing red, green, and blue light in order to create any color. You can choose any number between 0 and 255 for each of the three colors.
A few examples:
r = 0, g = 0, b = 0 is black
r = 255, g = 255, b = 255 is white
r = 255, g = 0, b = 0 is red

PRINT YOUR ART

Once your Python script has finished running and BEFORE you click on it (which will make it exit), print your screen and save your design. You can open your printed screen graphic with image-editing software and crop it to the size of the image. Print it out and share it with your friends!

```
from turtle import *            # imports the turtle module

from random import randint      # from the random module import the function randint
                                # like turtle it is a module, but this time we are only
                                    reading in one function, not all of them with *


speed(0)
bgcolor('black')

x = 0

while x < 400:                  # while the value of x is less than 120, continue

                                # create variables for r,g,b colors
    r = randint(0,255)          # set the variable to a random integer between 0 and 255
    g = randint(0,255)          # note: these numbers will change every time the loop runs
    b = randint(0,255)

    colormode(255)              # this tells Python to accept 3 integers: r,g,b for color

    pencolor(r,g,b)             # change the color of the pen to the r,g,b coordinates

    fd(50 + x)
    rt(105)                     # TAKE IT FURTHER: change this to rt(91)...or another number!

    x = x+1                     # adds 1 to the value of x

exitonclick()                   # when you click, turtle exits
```

HANDY TIP!
To print your artwork:
- On a Mac, capture the screen image using the basic keyboard shortcut of Command-Shift-3.
- On a PC, use the Printscreen button.

BECOME A FASHION DESIGNER

Fashion and technology have a growing relationship. From 3D-printing clothes to scanning bodies and making patterns, fashion is changing quickly with the help of code! Use your programming skills to create new patterns for using on your own fashion designs.

WHAT DOES A FASHION DESIGNER DO?

A fashion designer studies fashion trends and designs clothes, accessories, and shoes. Fashion designers sketch designs, create patterns for fabrics and styles, select materials, and take part in all the steps necessary for producing their designs. For this super skill, create your own fabric pattern using the skills you learned as an artist. You will then create a program to sketch designs.

FUNCTIONS

Functions, like loops, are helpful for defining things that you'd like to do over and over again. They are also useful for breaking your code into more manageable tasks. For example, imagine you have to draw many different people. On each person, each body part will be a different shape. If you had to draw each shape, one by one, your code would get very long, very quickly. Instead, if you defined how to draw a head, how to draw a body, and how to draw arms and legs, your code could be broken down into more manageable parts. Here's an example of what the code for your body parts would look like broken down:

```
def head:
    head here

def body:
    body here

def arms:
    arms here

def legs:
    legs here
```

To tie it all together, you can now write another function to draw a person.

```
def drawPerson:
    head ( )
    body ( )
    arms ( )
    legs ( )
```

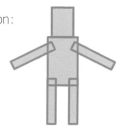

HANDY TIP!

You might notice that the code here isn't proper code. It's called **pseudocode** (pronounced sudo code). Pseudocode is similar to real code but is simplified and does not always have the correct punctuation. Programmers use it to quickly write down ideas. It is like writing an outline before writing the whole book.

Now, let's look at defining multiple functions in Python.

```python
from turtle import *                    # import the turtle module
from random import randint              # import randint from the random module

designer = Turtle()                     # declare Turtle as designer
designer.penup()                        # lift up the pen in order to move it to the correct place
designer.goto(-330,330)                 # send the designer to the top left corner

r, g, b = 0, 0, 0                       # create 3 numbers r, g, b to create colors
colormode(255)                          # set the color mode to 255

def chooseColor():                      # this function will choose a random color
    global r,g,b
    r = randint(0,255)
    g = randint(0,255)
    b = randint(0,255)

    designer.pencolor(r,g,b)            # set the pen color to the random color
    designer.fillcolor(r,g,b)           # set the fill color to the random color

    print ("Color is:", r, g, b)        # if this line of code is not needed, it can just be used for testing
                                        # it will print the color to the IDLE window for you to see

def drawSquare(size):                   # this function will draw a square
    designer.begin_fill()               # create a filled square
    designer.pendown()                  # set the pen down
    for i in range(4):                  # draw the square
        designer.forward(size)          # this will be the size of the square—try changing the number to change the size
        designer.right(90)
    designer.penup()                    # set the pen up so that you can move the designer
    designer.end_fill()

    print ("Square Drawn")              # this is also not needed, just used for testing

def drawOneRow(number, size):           # this function will draw a row of squares
    for i in range(number):             # draw 10 squares— number can be changed to make make more or fewer!
        chooseColor()                   # call the chooseColor() function to change the color each time the square is drawn
        drawSquare(size)                # draw a filled square
        designer.forward(size)          # move forward before drawing the next square
                                        # HINT: make sure this number is the same as the move forward amount in drawSquare()
                                        # you can test out different numbers to change the spacing

def drawPattern(number, size):          # this function will draw the final pattern
    for j in range(number):
        drawOneRow(number, size)        # draw ten rows and move down after each one
        designer.backward(size*number)  # work out how far back to move
        designer.right(90)
        designer.forward(size)
        designer.left(90)

drawPattern(10, 25)                     # call the function to draw your pattern
                                        # --> the first number is the number of squares
                                        # --> the second number is the size of the squares
```

CHANGING PATTERNS

Imagine you wanted to define something that might change each time, like the height of a person. Functions allow us to do this as well by **passing in** a requirement for our function to use. So, the drawPerson function might now say:

```
def drawPerson(height):
```

and if you called the function you could put in:

```
drawPerson(150)
```

Inside of the definition, you would tell the function how to handle the "height" by changing where the head, body, legs, and arms are drawn.

To explore this, we are going to work on our fashion pattern. Notice the updated code. Because we are passing in two numbers, we can now simply change these two numbers to update our pattern in:

drawPattern(number, size)

PASSING IN IS WHAT PROGRAMMERS CALL IT WHEN YOU TAKE SOMETHING FROM THE MAIN PART OF YOUR PROGRAM AND YOU PASS IT INTO A DEEPER LEVEL OF YOUR PROGRAM (SUCH AS A FUNCTION!).

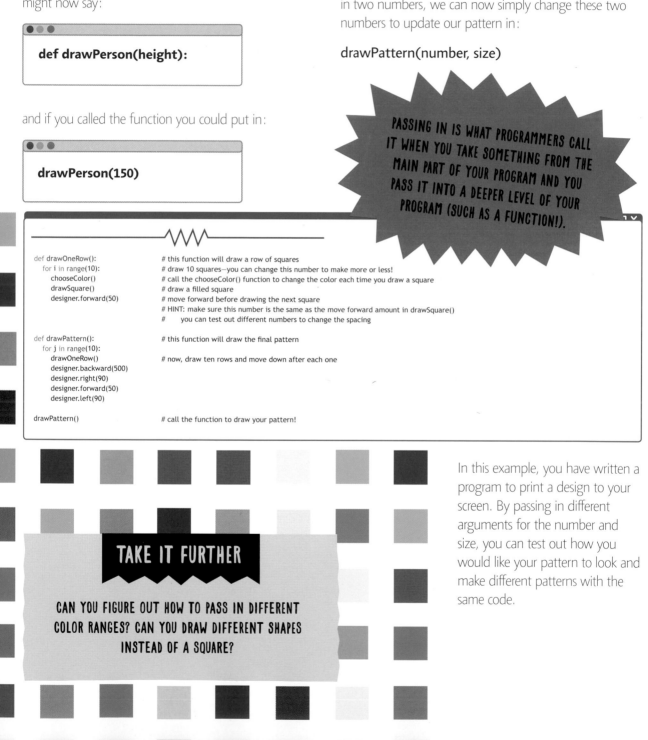

```
def drawOneRow():            # this function will draw a row of squares
    for i in range(10):       # draw 10 squares—you can change this number to make more or less!
        chooseColor()         # call the chooseColor() function to change the color each time you draw a square
        drawSquare()          # draw a filled square
        designer.forward(50)  # move forward before drawing the next square
                              # HINT: make sure this number is the same as the move forward amount in drawSquare()
                              #       you can test out different numbers to change the spacing

def drawPattern():           # this function will draw the final pattern
    for j in range(10):
        drawOneRow()          # now, draw ten rows and move down after each one
        designer.backward(500)
        designer.right(90)
        designer.forward(50)
        designer.left(90)

drawPattern()                # call the function to draw your pattern!
```

In this example, you have written a program to print a design to your screen. By passing in different arguments for the number and size, you can test out how you would like your pattern to look and make different patterns with the same code.

TAKE IT FURTHER

CAN YOU FIGURE OUT HOW TO PASS IN DIFFERENT COLOR RANGES? CAN YOU DRAW DIFFERENT SHAPES INSTEAD OF A SQUARE?

DESIGN IT

Now that you have figured out what you would like your pattern to look like, let's design with it!

○ Print out your pattern as you did with your spirograph drawing. (See page 23.)

○ Draw a piece of clothing, such as a dress, a shirt, or a tie, on a white piece of paper or find a design from a magazine.

○ Cut out your drawing or magazine design.

○ Trace around the cut-out design on the front of your pattern printout.

  ○ Cut out your design from the pattern paper and you're done. You're a real fashion designer!

HANDY TIP!
You can also cut out a piece of clothing from a magazine or print one from the computer to cut out.

LET'S CLICK

We are going to use a new **module** that is similar to Turtle, called **Tkinter**. Tkinter is Python's built-in **GUI** module. GUI stands for graphical user interface and it is pronounced "gooey." You can think of it as the screen you interact with when communicating with the computer. It is made up of images, buttons, and text.

Let's take a look at the Tkinter module with this program below:

Here is an example of the **output** when the program is run:

```
_ □ X

Clicked at: 43 48
Clicked at: 26 24
Clicked at: 85 27
Clicked at: 91 81
Clicked at: 3 84
Clicked at: 3 3
Clicked at: 97 98
Clicked at: 85 53
Clicked at: 41 71
```

```
_ □ X

from tkinter import *                                           # import the tkinter GUI module

def main():                                                     # this is the main function of your program
    root = Tk()                                                 # initialize tkinter root
    myWindow = Canvas(root, width=100, height=100)              # name your canvas myWindow and set the size to 100 x 100
    myWindow.pack()
    myWindow.bind("<Button-1>", testClick)                      # this is where you will bind <Button-1> to a new event handler called testClick
    root.mainloop()                                             # starts the main event loop

def testClick(event):
    print ("Clicked at:", event.x, event.y)                    # define the testClick event handler and what to do when it occurs

main()                                                          # start the mainloop by calling the main() function!
```

EVENTS

In this program, we will add a new piece to your super skill: an **event**. An event in programming is something that happens while a program is running—for example, moving the mouse, clicking a button, or typing on a keyboard.

In order to check for these events, we attach the events to event handlers to tell the program what to do when the event happens. You can think of **event handlers** as similar to functions. The only difference is you are passing in events instead of **variables** (see page 34).

So, in this case, we bind (attach) the button click to tell us which **coordinate** on the canvas was clicked!

THE EVENT.X AND EVENT.Y RELATE TO THE X AND Y COORDINATES ON THE TKINTER WINDOW. THE COORDINATES ARE MAPPED TO THE POSITION OF THE PIXELS.

MAIN LOOP

A Tkinter program uses an **"event"** loop, which continually checks what's happening and looks for events that the user is giving to the computer. If an event matching one of the descriptions in the program occurs, the "event" loop sends the "event" handler information about the event.

THE -1 IN "<BUTTON-PRESS-1>" STANDS FOR THE LEFT CLICK.

```
from tkinter import *                                      # import the tkinter GUI module

myPen = "up"                                               # create your pen
myX, myY = None, None                                      # set the X and Y position to None

def main():
    root = Tk()                                            # initialize tkinter root
    mySketch = Canvas(root)                                # name your canvas mySketch; can you remember how to set the size of the canvas to 600 x 600?
    mySketch.pack()
    mySketch.bind("<Motion>", motion)                      # motion is your mouse movement
    mySketch.bind("<ButtonPress-1>", myPenDown)            # myPenDown is when you hold down the left mouse button
    mySketch.bind("<ButtonRelease-1>", myPenUp)            # myPenUp is when you release the left mouse button
    root.mainloop()                                        # starts the main event loop

def myPenDown(event):                                      # define what should happen when your pen is down
    global myPen                                           # tells the myPenDown definition that we will be using the myPen variable
    myPen = "down"                                         # you only want to draw when the button is down
                                                           # because the "<Motion>" events happen all the time

def myPenUp(event):                                        # define what should happen when your pen is up
    global myPen, myX, myY                                 # tells the myPenUp definition that we will be using these variables
    myPen = "up"                                           # you don't want to draw when the button is up
    myX = None                                             # reset the line start when you let go of the button
    myY = None

def motion(event):                                         # define what to do when your mouse is in motion
    global myX, myY
    if myPen == "down":                                    # only draw if your pen is "down"
        if myX is not None and myY is not None:            # here's where you draw your sketch!
            event.widget.create_line(myX,myY,event.x,event.y,smooth=TRUE)
        myX = event.x
        myY = event.y

main()                                                     # now that all of your events are defined, call main() to start the program
```

In this program, we are binding the **<ButtonPress-1>** event to tell the pen to start drawing, the **<ButtonRelease-1>** event to tell the pen to stop drawing and reset the drawing coordinates, and, finally, the **<Motion>** event to tell the program how to draw the line.

Congratulations, you can now sketch like a real fashion designer!

HANDY TIP!
Notice the event is in green and has "< and >" around it to tell Python it is an event.

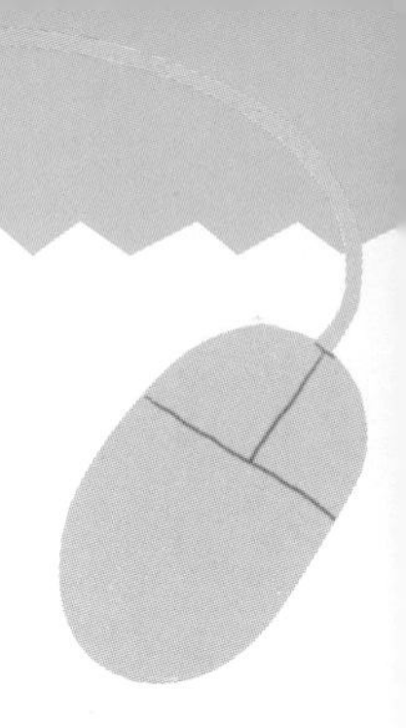

BECOME AN ARCHITECT

Architects design all kinds of buildings and spaces for people to live, work, and play in. Before these buildings and spaces can be built, architects need to draw their designs in order for construction workers to know what to build and how to build it. Architects do a lot of this work on computers. They use code to help them design as well as to help them automate processes and tasks they do over and over again. With this super skill, you will learn how to design a skyscraper using code!

We are going to use **Tkinter** again to design a skyscraper. Tkinter has its own built-in **function** for drawing rectangles. This is called:

create_rectangle

and it takes the following **inputs**:

(x1, y1, x2, y2, outline, fill)

Notice how drawing a rectangle in this case is done by telling the computer that the two (x,y) **coordinates** are located in the top left and bottom right corners.

CAN YOU EXPLAIN HOW USING THESE INPUTS IS DIFFERENT FROM WHEN YOU DREW A SQUARE WITH TURTLE?

In order to draw a skyscraper, we will use a similar approach as we did with the fashion pattern of squares. This time, however, we will draw rectangles in a grid. The rectangles will represent windows. We will also need to leave a gap between the windows, to represent the structure of our skyscraper.

NESTED "FOR" LOOP

Instead of drawing one row at a time and then moving down, we can use a very handy programming concept called a **nested loop**. This simply means that one loop is placed inside another loop.

It looks like this in **pseudocode**:

for i in range(winW):
    for j in range(winH):
        draw rectangle

In this example, winW is the number of windows wide and winH is the number of windows high, as you can see from the diagram below.

	j = 0	j = 1	j = 2	j = 3	j = 4
i = 0	0	1	2	3	4
i = 1	5	6	7	8	9
i = 2	10	11	12	13	14
i = 3	15	16	17	18	19
i = 4	20	21	22	23	24

PROPORTION

Proportion is an important part of architectural design, creating a connection between mathematics and art. It refers to the relative size and scale of different elements in a design. For example, the width of the windows compared to the height of the windows and the gap between the windows creates a window-to-building proportion in the skyscraper. If we change the number of windows across or the number of windows high, we would change the proportion. Changing the proportion impacts the visual effect of your design!

```
from tkinter import *

def newSkyscraper():                              # try changing the following 5 numbers and then re-running your program to design your skyscraper!
    winW = 10                                     # set the number of windows wide
    winH = 15                                     # set the number of windows high
    w = 15                                        # set the width of the windows
    h = 20                                        # set the height of the windows
    gap = 2                                       # set the window gap

                                                                              # draw the main building
    myBuilding.create_rectangle(gap,gap,(winW+2)*gap+winW*w,(winH+2)*gap+winH*h,    # startX(left),startY(top),finishX(right),finishY(bottom)
                        outline="gray", fill="gray")                          # outline and fill colors

                                                                              # draw windows
    for i in range(winW):
        for j in range(winH):
            myBuilding.create_rectangle(((w+gap)*i+2*gap),                    # startX(left)
                        ((h+gap)*j+2*gap),                                    # startY(top)
                        ((w+gap)*i+(2*gap+w)),                                # finishX(right)
                        ((h+gap)*j+(2*gap+h)),                                # finishY(bottom)
                        outline="black",fill="white")                         # outline, fill colors
                                                                              # try using different colors such as "blue" or "red"
    myBuilding.pack(fill=BOTH, expand=1)                                      # add ALL of the rectangles to your Canvas

""" Main Program """
root = Tk()                                                                   # set up Tkinter
myBuilding = Canvas(root, width=500, height=500)                             # set up Canvas
root.title("Skyscraper")                                                      # set the title of your screen
myBuilding.pack()                                                             # pack adds everything to the Tkinter Canvas

""" Draw Button """
button = Button(root, text="Draw Skyscraper", command=newSkyscraper)        # create a button to draw the skyscraper
button.pack()                                                                 # add it to the Canvas

root.mainloop()                                                              # start the main loop
```

Try changing the five **variables** (see page 34) in your code.

winW   # Number of windows wide
winH   # Number of windows high
w   # Window width
h   # Window height
gap   # The gap between the windows (You might think of this as the structure)

Once you've changed the variable numbers, try running your code again.

Congratulations, you've designed your first skyscraper!

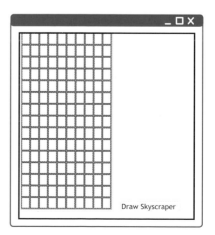

Draw Skyscraper

BUILDING A PARAMETRIC MODEL

It's not very efficient to keep having to change the numbers in your code in order to design the skyscraper. Instead, you can add scales (also known as sliders) to your program to make it easier. The scales will let you choose different numbers while the skyscraper program is still running.

We need to add a scale for each of the five variables. Once the scales are drawn in your program, the user can update the scale numbers and push the "draw skyscraper" button. The code will then automatically redraw the skyscraper with the new proportions.

In architecture, this is called a parametric model. It simply means a model that has **parameters** which can be changed. A model in architecture is the representation of the building being designed. This could be a drawing, like your drawing on the screen, or a physical model that you might build out of cardboard. A parameter is like a variable that allows us to pass information or instructions into functions and procedures. They are very useful for numeric information such as stating the size of an object. In this case, we are stating the size and number of windows as well as the space between the windows.

Now, let's update your skyscraper by creating a parametric model using sliders.

```
from tkinter import *
def newSkyscraper():
        winW = scaleWinW.get()                                    # get the number of windows wide from the scale
        winH = scaleWinH.get()                                    # get the number of windows high from the scale
        w = scaleW.get()                                          # get the width of the windows from the scale
        h = scaleH.get()                                          # get the height of the windows from the scale
        gap = scaleGap.get()                                      # get the window gap from the scale

        myBuilding.delete("all")                                  # this will clear the drawing before drawing new squares

                                                                  # draw main building
        myBuilding.create_rectangle(gap,gap,(winW+2)*gap+winW*w,(winH+2)*gap+winH*h,   # startX(left),startY(top),finishX(right),finishY(bottom)
                          outline="gray", fill="gray")            # outline and fill colors

     for i in range(winW):                                        # draw windows
         for j in range(winH):
             myBuilding.create_rectangle(((w+gap)*i+2*gap),       # startX(left)
                         ((h+gap)*j+2*gap),                       # startY(top)
                         ((w+gap)*i+(2*gap+w)),                   # finishX(right)
                         ((h+gap)*j+(2*gap+h)),                   # finishY(bottom)
                         outline="black",fill="white")            # outline, fill colors
                                                                  # try using different colors such as 'blue" or "red"
        myBuilding.pack(fill=BOTH, expand=1)                      # add ALL of the rectangles to your Canvas
""" Main Program """
root = Tk()                                                       # set up Tkinter
myBuilding = Canvas(root, width=500, height=500)                  # set up Canvas
root.title("Skyscraper")                                          # set the title of your screen
myBuilding.pack()                                                 # pack adds everything to the Tkinter Canvas
""" Draw Scales """
scaleWinW = Scale(root, from_=5, to=30, orient=HORIZONTAL, label= "Windows Wide")   # create a scale for the number of windows wide
scaleWinW.pack()                                                  # add it to the Canvas
                                      # HINT: you can copy the above two lines for the next 4 scales and simply change the variable names
scaleWinH = Scale(root, from_=5, to=30, orient=HORIZONTAL, label= "Windows High")   # create a scale for the number of windows high
scaleWinH.pack()                                                  # add it to the Canvas

scaleW = Scale(root, from_=5, to=30, orient=HORIZONTAL, label= "Window Width")      # create a scale for the windows' width
scaleW.pack()                                                     # add it to the Canvas

scaleH = Scale(root, from_=5, to=30, orient=HORIZONTAL, label= "Window Height")     # create a scale for the windows' height
scaleH.pack()                                                     # add it to the Canvas

scaleGap = Scale(root, from_=2, to=20, orient=HORIZONTAL, label= "Window Gap")      # create a scale for the size of the gap between windows
scaleGap.pack()                                                   # did you notice the smaller numbers for the from_ and to?
""" Draw Button """
button = Button(root, text= "Draw Skyscraper", command=newSkyscraper)               # create a button to draw the skyscraper
button.pack()                                                     # add it to the Canvas

root.mainloop()                                                   # start the main loop
```

Examples of the **output** and how you can change the look of your skyscraper are here. Can you also change the color of your skyscraper? What other things can you think of to add to the design?

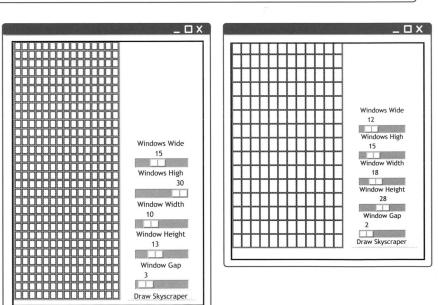

BECOME A SPY

Coding languages, such as Python, encode information that computers can use and understand. But what exactly does encoding mean? To better understand, this super skill will have you create and decipher secret messages using different ciphers, putting your skills to the test!

WHAT IS A SPY?

A spy operates in the world of espionage. Espionage is the process of obtaining information that is not normally publicly available by using human sources (agents) or technical means (like hacking into computer systems). Spies blend into their surroundings and collect valuable information (often called intelligence). Many agencies have been set up around the world, such as the CIA, MI6, HVA, the KGB, and Interpol. Do you know which agency operates in your country?

VARIABLES

Part of being a spy is disguising information. Programming languages have a handy tool used for disguising information. These are called **variables** and are used to store information such as numbers, words, or lists. You can think of them as labels that describe what you're storing. For example, if you were a spy and had labels for all of the things that describe a dog named Griffin, you might store them like this:

Type the below into the **IDLE** window:

```
name = "Griffin" # "name" is a variable
age = 2
color = "black"
magic words  = "eat", "sleep", "walk", "play"
tricks = "sit", "stay", "speak", "paw"
isHappy = True
```

After you've typed the above code, test out your variables by typing any of the words into IDLE (such as **>>> age** or **>>> tricks**). It will return the information you have stored in the variable!

Variables are useful, especially when the information you're storing in them might need to change. For example, if Griffin just had a birthday, you could type:

```
age = 3  # this now changes age from 2 to 3
```

You could also write:

```
age += 1  # this will add 1 to age
```

USE THE = SYMBOL TO ASSIGN THE INFORMATION TO OUR VARIABLE.

MAGIC WORDS

Spies also use secret code to communicate with each other for secrecy or convenience. For example, projects might be identified by a secret code word.

Unlike human languages, the Python vocabulary is actually quite small. We call this vocabulary the reserved words. These are words that have very special meaning to Python, like secret code words do to spies. These "magic" words are how a function is defined, or how an instruction is given. When Python sees these words in a Python program, they have one and only one meaning to Python. This means that we aren't allowed to use them as variable names, but can use them for instructions.

The best example is to think of Python as a dog. It has already been trained to listen to the reserved words. For a real dog these might be "sit", "stay", or "paw". When you speak to your dog and don't use the reserved words, they just look at you adoringly. For example, if you say, "Are you going to stay in town for the holidays?", what your dog would hear is: "Blah blah blah blah stay blah blah blah blah blah?"

PYTHON'S RESERVED WORDS

False   class   is   finally   return   None

continue   for   try   lambda   True   def

from   nonlocal   while   and   del   global

not   if   as   elif   with   or   yield   assert

else   import   pass   break   except   in   raise

That's it. Unlike a dog, Python is already completely trained. When you say, "try," Python will try every time you say it, no matter what!

CIPHER

The use of codes (or ciphers) for hiding the meaning of messages traces its roots to ancient history. The first known military use of codes was by Julius Caesar in 60–50 BC. Because of this, a cipher was created and named after him. We will use both paper and code to create our own Caesar cipher to understand how coding languages work.

CAESAR CIPHER

The Caesar cipher shifts the letters in the alphabet by a certain number of letters as a way to generate a new alphabet. Each letter in the original alphabet is then substituted by its corresponding letter in the new shifted alphabet.

The Caesar cipher specified that each letter in the alphabet would be encoded using the letter three positions later in the alphabet. For example, "a"

would be encoded as "d", "b" would be encoded as "e", "c" would be encoded as "f", and so on. The code wraps around at the end of the alphabet, so "x", "y", and "z" would be encoded as "a", "b", and "c", respectively. The complete mapping of letters is shown below.

a b c d e f g h i j k l m n o p q r s t u v w x y z

d e f g h i j k l m n o p q r s t u v w x y z a b c

Let's say your favorite number is 3 and you use 3 as your "key." You will then shift the alphabet three spaces. A becomes D, B becomes E, C becomes F, and so on. When you get to the end of the alphabet, simply wrap the alphabet around again, turning X into A, Y into B, and Z into C.

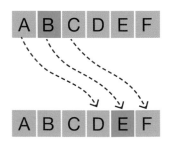

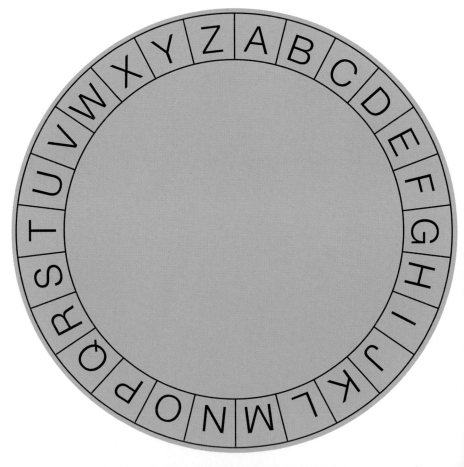

CIPHER VS CODE

Codes are made to be understandable and publicly available. Anyone should be able to look up what a code's symbols mean to decode an encoded message. Ciphers, on the other hand, are created to convert plain text into cipher text with a secret key or code word.

MAKE A PAPER CIPHER WHEEL

Let's create a tool to practice encrypting and decrypting plain text and cipher text. For this we will create something called a cipher wheel or cipher disk.

○ Photocopy these two pages and cut out the two circles. (Don't cut out the pages from this book!)
○ Place the smaller circle in the middle of the larger one.
○ Put a brad or pin through the center of both circles so that you can spin them around in place.

Now you have a tool for creating secret messages with the Caesar cipher!

ENCRYPT A MESSAGE

To encrypt a secret message, first line up your cipher wheel so that A matches with A.

Let's use the key 6 to send the message "**Meet me at the white house in one hour.**"

○ Turn the outer circle of your cipher wheel 6 spaces clockwise so that A on the outside lines up with G6 on the inside.
○ For each letter in your message, write down the corresponding letter from the inner circle.
○ So M becomes S, E becomes K, and so on.

Your plain text has now become a new encrypted cipher text which reads:

Skkz sk gz znk cnozk nuayk ot utk nuax - 6

The "6" in the message gives your receiver the key for decrypting your message. The Caesar cipher can only have a key from 0 to 25. (The wheel wouldn't move with key 0, though, so we wouldn't want to use that!)

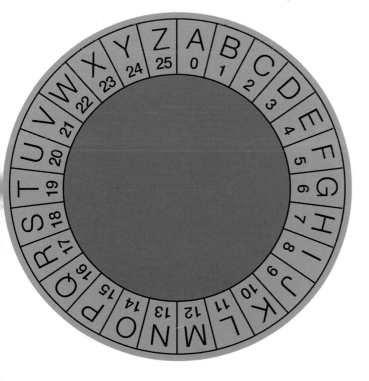

TAKE IT FURTHER

TRY DECRYPTING THIS MESSAGE:
DRO AESMU LBYGX PYH TEWZC YFOB
DRO VKJI NYQC – 10
AS YOU CAN SEE, THIS WOULD BE QUITE TEDIOUS TO DO BY HAND IF YOU HAD A LONG MESSAGE. THIS IS WHERE OUR PROGRAMMING SKILLS COME IN HANDY!

A SPY ON THE RUN

Imagine you are a spy. You've just found the location of a diamond that is bigger than any ever before seen on Earth. The only problem is you are now on the run, you can't let anyone know you've found the diamond—trust no one. Your only hope is to communicate with the head of your spy agency, Sam, in order to secure the diamond and ensure your safety. Create a program to both encode and decode messages using a Caesar cipher in order to communicate with Sam!

CODING A CAESAR CIPHER

Here's what you need to know.

- The key is an **integer** from 1 to 25.
- This cipher rotates (either left or right) the letters of the alphabet (A to Z).

- The encoding replaces each letter with the 1st to 25th next letter in the alphabet (wrapping Z to A).

Great! Now encode the following message to send to Sam:

KEY 2 ENCRYPTS "HI" TO "JK"; BUT KEY 20 ENCRYPTS "HI" TO "BC".

> **I found the diamond it is in Antarctica send help**

```
# t is the text string for decoding/encoding
# k is the key integer
# decode is a boolean
def caesar(t, k, decode = False):       # check if you are decoding or encoding
        if decode: k = 26 - k           # if decode = True, shift the key forward to 26—the key amount
                                        # (returning it to its original position)

        return "".join([chr((ord(i) - 65 + k) % 26 + 65)    # the math behind shifting our letters
                for i in t.upper()                          # for every letter in the text
                if ord(i) >= 65 and ord(i) <= 90 ])         # check if the character is a letter between A and Z
                                                            # test the code
                                                            # change the text and key to test different messages
text = "The quick brown fox jumped over the lazy dogs"
key = 11

encr = caesar(text, key)
decr = caesar(encr, key, decode = True)

print (text)
print (encr)                            # Output:
print (decr)                            #   Plain text = The quick brown fox jumped over the lazy dogs
                                        #   Encrypted text = ESPBFTNVMCZHYQZIUFXAPOZGPCESPWLKJOZRD
                                        #   Decrypted text = THEQUICKBROWNFOXJUMPEDOVERTHELAZYDOGS
```

A MORE ADVANCED CIPHER

Oh dear! Your code has fallen into the hands of an enemy and they can decode your simple cipher. Don't worry, you can create a more complex cipher in order to avoid being detected. Using a Vigenère cipher you will add a code word to the cipher instead of just a simple number. Here's how it works.

The Vigenère cypher is similar to the Caesar cipher, except with multiple keys. The key in a Vigenère cipher is like a code word. This single word key will be split into multiple subkeys. If you use a Vigenère key of "HELLO," then the

first subkey is "H", the second subkey is "E", the third and fourth subkeys are both "L", and the fifth subkey is "O." You can then use the first subkey to encrypt the first letter of the plain text, and the second subkey to encrypt the second letter, and so on. When we get to the sixth letter of the plain text, we will go back to using the first.

Encoding messages is important for a spy and for programming. Now that you have a better understanding of how encoding and decoding work, you are one step closer to mastering Python.

Try out the Vigenère code below:

```
from itertools import starmap, cycle
def encrypt(message, key):

    message = filter(str.isalpha, message.upper())        # convert to uppercase

    def enc(c,k): return chr(((ord(k) + ord(c) - 2*ord('A')) % 26) + ord('A'))    # strip out non-alpha characters

    return "".join(starmap(enc, zip(message, cycle(key))))    # single letter encryption

def decrypt(message, key):

    def dec(c,k): return chr(((ord(c) - ord(k) - 2*ord('A')) % 26) + ord('A'))    # single letter decryption

    return "".join(starmap(dec, zip(message, cycle(key))))

text = "Hello everyone, I love to code and am training to be a spy!"    # test the code:
key = "VIGENERECIPHER"

encr = encrypt(text, key)
decr = decrypt(encr, key)

print (text)
print (encr)
print (decr)

# Output:
#   Plain text = Hello everyone, I love to code and am training to be a spy!
#   Encrypted text = CMRPBIMITGDUIZGWBIGSTSFMPUHRHBXEVRZRIBDIIRNXE
#   Decrypted text = HELLOEVERYONEILOVETOCODEANDAMTRAININGTOBEASPY
```

BECOME A TEACHER

In this super skill, we will explore how to use files in your programs. Teachers have to do many organizational tasks for their students on a regular basis. In this chapter, you will learn how to organize students and write a quiz program using Python.

READING FROM A FILE

Let's start with reading from a file. For this example, we are using a text file that contains a list of different animals starting with the letter B. You can download our file from **GitHub** (https://github.com/elizabethtweedale/HowToCode2) or you can open a text editor document and type in the first ten names you can think of in any order. To read from a file, you need to first open the file, then use a **"for" loop** to go over each line of the file. See below.

```
with open("b-animals.txt", mode="r", encoding="utf-8") as myFile:
    for line in myFile:
        print(line)
```

In addition to the filename, "open" takes two other **parameters**. The first one is mode. This determines what you can do with the file once it has been opened. There are three main options:

- r — open the file for reading
- w — open the file for writing (This deletes all existing content if the file already exists.)
- a — open the file to append data to it (Appending the data will just add more data to the end of the file, without deleting the data that already exists.)

The second parameter is encoding. This determines how the characters will be encoded (just like we did as a spy)

into the computer language. It is best to use "utf-8" as it works on Windows, Mac, and Linux. ("utf-8" is character encoding, which uses 8-bit blocks to represent characters.)

NEWLINE

You might notice that Python prints an extra line each time it moves to a new line in your text document. A handy trick to remove the new line character (**"\n"**) from your text file is to "strip" the newline characters from your file. **rstrip** removes whitespace from the right-hand side of the string and **lstrip** removes it from the left-hand side. See below.

```
with open("B-Animals.txt", mode="r", encoding="utf-8") as myFile:
    for line in myFile:
        print(line.rstrip("\n"))
```

READING INTO A LIST

Now that we have read in data from a file, it would be useful to store it in a list so that we can use it later (instead of just printing it to the screen!). This is similar to creating a new **variable** and can be done simply with the following code.

```
with open("B-Animals.txt", mode="r", encoding="utf-8") as myFile:
    animals = myFile.read().splitlines()
print(animals)
```

The **read()** method reads the entire file and uses the **splitlines function** to separate the lines of the file and remove the newline character from the end of each line. Once the lines are separated, the function places them in a list.

WRITING TO A FILE

Next, we will look at how to write to a file. As we've just used the **read()** mode, we will now simply use the **write()** method. To write information to a file, first you need to open the file, then use the **write()** method to write to it. If the file you are writing to does not exist, Python will create a new .txt file and then write to the new file.

```
animals = ["badger","buffalo","bear"]
with open("newAnimals.txt", mode="w",encoding="utf-8") as myFile:
    for animal in animals:
        myFile.write(animal+"\n")
```

BUBBLE SORT

As a teacher, you will need to sort people's names into alphabetical order. Now that you're comfortable reading and writing text files, you can read in from a file, use a simple **algorithm** called **bubbleSort** to sort the list of names, and then write the newly sorted list into a file.

```
def bubbleSort(unsorted):
    noSwaps = True
    while noSwaps:
        noSwaps = False
        for item in range(0,len(unsorted)-1):
            if unsorted[item] > unsorted[item+1]:
                temp = unsorted[item+1]
                unsorted[item+1] = unsorted[item]
                unsorted[item] = temp
                noSwaps = True

with open("studentsUnsorted.txt",mode="r",encoding="utf-8") as myFile:
    students = myFile.read().splitlines()

bubbleSort(students)

with open("studentsSorted.txt",mode="w",encoding="utf-8") as myFile:
    for student in students:
        myFile.write(student+"\n")
```

THE TEACHER'S QUIZ

Let's write a program to test students on their Python knowledge! In order to do this, we will use some of the things we have learned in our super skills to brush up on our own knowledge as well.

So far we have used text files. Another file type which is very useful for storing and reading simple data is a CSV file. CSV file formats are used to store table data such as spreadsheets or databases but can also easily be read in text documents.

THE PLAN FOR YOUR QUIZ CODE

◦ Start by asking for the student's name, so we know who is taking the test.

◦ The questions are stored in a CSV file along with the answers.

◦ Open the CSV file that contains questions and answers in it.

◦ Ask the student the questions one at a time.

◦ Record the student's answer and tell them if they are right or wrong. You can also tell them the correct answer if they get it wrong.

◦ At the end, we can tell the student what their score is and write their name and score to the class file.

◦ The quiz will run in the IDLE window where the user can type in their answers.

CSV stands for Comma Separated Values, where each piece of data is separated by a comma. So be careful to not use commas in the data you're storing in CSV files! For example, if you were storing this sentence in a CSV file: "Python is a language used in programming, and it is also the name of a reptile," it would not be stored as a single item, but as two separate items.

```python
import csv, random
def askName():                                          # askName function returns the name of the student
    print("Welcome to the Super Python Quiz!")
    yourName = input("What is your name? ")
    print ("Hello",str(yourName))
    return yourName

def getQuestions():                                     # getQuestions reads in the questions from a CSV file
    questions = []                                      # this creates an empty list for adding the questions to
    with open("SuperPythonQuiz.csv", mode="r", encoding="utf-8") as myFile:
    myQuiz = csv.reader(myFile)
    for row in myQuiz:
        questions.append(row)
    return questions

def askQuestion(question,score):                        # askQuestion prints the question and choices to the screen then checks the answer
    print(question[0])                                  # print the question—this is in the [0] position of the row
    for eachChoice in question[1:-1]:                   # print each choice from [1] to the last position [-1]
        print("{0:>5}{1}".format("", eachChoice))
    answer = input("Please select an answer: ")         # get the student's answer
    if answer == question[-1]:                          # check if the answer matches the last position in the question, the correct answer
        print("Correct!")                               # if it's correct, tell the user and add one to the score
        score += 1
    else:                                               # if it's incorrect, tell the user what the correct answer was
        print("Incorrect, the correct answer was {0}.".format(question[-1]))
    return score                                        # return the score

def recordScore(studentName, score):
    with open("QuizResults.txt", mode="a+",encoding="utf-8") as myFile:   # note the "+" sign after the "a" means if the file does not exist, then create it
        myFile.write(str(studentName) + "," + str(score) + "\n")          # write name, score to the file
                                                        # "\n" will add a new line to the file so that it's ready for the next name

def main():
    studentName = askName()                             # call the askName function
    questions = getQuestions()                          # call the getQuestions function
    score = 0                                           # initialize the score to 0

    number = len(questions)                             # use the number to keep track of the total number of questions—which is the length of the "questions" list
    for eachQuestion in range(number):                  # repeat for each question
        question = random.choice(questions)             # choose a random question from the questions list
        score = askQuestion(question,score)             # ask the question and update the score
        questions.remove(question)                      # remove the current question from the list so that you don't ask it again

    print("Your final score is:", score, "out of:", number)   # tell the user what their final score is
    recordScore(studentName, score)                     # call the recordScore function

main()
```

DATA TYPES

You might have noticed that when we were writing to the student file, we used the **str() function**. This function converts anything inside the parentheses into a string. A string is made up of a string of characters—which is what text files have in them. We have to use it to write the score into our file because the score is an integer (also known as a whole number).

These values, such as studentName, score, and the other variables we have used in our programs, are known as data types.

- type str: belongs to strings—anything inside parentheses is a string

- type int : belongs to integers

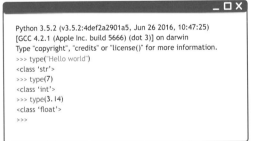

```
Python 3.5.2 (v3.5.2:4def2a2901a5, Jun 26 2016, 10:47:25)
[GCC 4.2.1 (Apple Inc. build 5666) (dot 3)] on darwin
Type "copyright", "credits" or "license()" for more information.
>>> type("Hello world")
<class 'str'>
>>> type(7)
<class 'int'>
>>> type(3.14)
<class 'float'>
>>>
```

- type float: belongs to floating point numbers (numbers with decimal points in them like 3.14)

If you are not sure what type a value has, the Python Interpreter can tell you!

BECOME A MUSICIAN

As in so many other professions, the music industry is being transformed by technology, from digital synthesizers and software that teaches you to play musical instruments to algorithms that write music based on a set of rules. In this super skill, we will look at adding sounds to our programs. We will also start using graphic images and create our own digital soundboard for playing and creating music.

Electronic and digital music technology is the use of computers, electronic effects units, software, or digital audio equipment by a musician, composer, sound engineer, DJ, or record producer to make, perform, or record music.

Music technology is connected to both artistic and technological creativity. Musicians and music technology experts are trying to make new ways of expressing themselves through music, and they are creating new devices and software to enable them to do so.

SOUNDS

A soundboard is a computer program that stores and plays different sound bites (short sounds or notes played on recorded instruments) and audio clips (like voice recordings or songs). The great thing about a soundboard is that it can play the sounds it stores on its own without a media player like iTunes, QuickTime, Windows Media Player, or a CD player.

In order to create your own soundboard program using sounds and images, you need to install a useful library called **Pygame**.

TWISTEDWAVE.COM IS A COOL WEBSITE THAT CAN RECORD OR EDIT ANY AUDIO FILE.

HANDY TIP!
Here's another great resource for instructions on how to download and install pygame for Mac or Windows: http://kidscancode.org/blog/2015/09/pygame_install

INSTALL PYGAME

Pygame is a cross-platform library, meaning it can be used on different operating systems like Windows or Mac. It's even built into the Raspberry Pi! Pygame is designed to make it easy to write multimedia software, such as games, in Python.

You might remember that Python comes with its own library of **modules**, such as Turtle. By installing Pygame, you will be adding a second library with many more useful modules to work with Python. Pygame is particularly good at using sounds and images, which will be perfect for this super skill.

Let's start by downloading and installing Pygame.

○ Go to: http://www.pygame.org/download.shtml

○ Choose the Source that is correct for your operating system (Windows, Mac, or Linux).

○ Download the installation file and open the downloaded file.

○ Proceed to install the Pygame software on your computer. Refer to the Pygame website if you need help installing.

○ You will not be able to install Pygame from IDLE. You will need to run the installation from the Command line using Terminal (or Command Prompt). After Pygame is installed properly, you can use IDLE again.

HANDY TIP!
In order to successfully open your first program, your HelloWorld.py program file must be saved in your main folder (C:/ in Windows or the User folder on a Mac).

OPEN YOUR PYTHON SCRIPTS FROM THE COMMAND LINE

To give instructions using the Command line, we can simply type them in as we did in IDLE, but this time using the Terminal (in Mac) or Command Prompt (in Windows). Programmers use the Command line because it's the simplest way to communicate directly with the operating system of your computer. This means you're not talking to your computer through another program. (See page 13 for a reminder of what we learned about the CPU.)

Open the Command line on your computer using the Command Prompt in Windows or Terminal on a Mac.

Type:

```
python3
>>> import pygame
```

You should now see:

```
>>>
```

If you do, then congratulations! You have installed Pygame successfully.

Now try opening the first program you wrote: HelloWorld.py. Type:

```
python3 : Python/HelloWorld.py
```

SOUND

In order to add sounds to your program, you first need to find a sound. You can either use one of the sounds from GitHub (https://github.com/elizabethtweedale/HowToCode2) or find your own from these websites:

www.opengameart.org
www.freesound.org

Sound files come in many different file types. The extension after the file name will tell you what kind of file type you are downloading. Here are some examples.

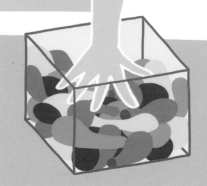

○ **mySound.wav**: wav is short for Waveform Audio File. Wav files are usually larger than other files because most of them are uncompressed.

○ **mySound.mp3**: a very popular file format which stores sound files in small sizes. Most digital devices that can play sound can read and play .mp3 files.

○ **mySound.ogg**: an ogg file format creates better quality sounds than some other compressed file types. For Pygame, an .ogg file is the most reliable.

Let's write our first Pygame program. Before this code will work, you need to either download the whirl.ogg file or one of your own files and replace the name of the file in your code.

COMPRESSED VS UNCOMPRESSED

Think of a .wav file as a room full of one million balloons. This would be an uncompressed file. Now imagine if you took the air out of the balloons and packed them away into a very small box—this would be a compressed file, like an .mp3 or .ogg file. Ogg files are good at taking the air out of the balloons but keeping them most like a balloon!

```
import pygame                                          # import Pygame—load all of the pygame resources
pygame.init()                                          # initialize Pygame—setting it up
screen = pygame.display.set_mode([400, 400])           # set the screen size to 400 x 400 pixels—try changing these numbers and see how it updates
pygame.display.set_caption('Super Skills')             # set the caption of your screen to anything you like, ours is called 'Super Skills'
click_sound = pygame.mixer.Sound("whirl.ogg")          # label your sound and load in the file—you can call 'click_sound' anything you like
soundboard = True                                      # this is a boolean (True/False), which tells our program to continue—it can also be named anything
while soundboard:
    for event in pygame.event.get():                   # this is the main drawing event loop of the program. It captures any events that will happen
        if event.type == pygame.QUIT:                  # if the user quits the program, tell the program to stop
            soundboard = False
        elif event.type == pygame.MOUSEBUTTONDOWN:     # if the user clicks the mouse...
            click_sound.play()                         # play the sound loaded in
print ("Goodbye Soundboard!")                          # print to the IDLE screen when you exit
pygame.quit()                                          # quit Pygame
```

After running your code, click anywhere to play the sound!

COPYRIGHT
- - - - - - -
IT IS IMPORTANT TO ONLY USE OPEN SOURCE SOUNDS. MUSIC THAT HAS A COPYRIGHT SHOULD NOT BE USED EVEN TO TEST YOUR CODE. EVEN IF YOU MAKE A VIDEO OF YOUR PROGRAM WITH THE COPYRIGHT SONG IN THE BACKGROUND. WEBSITES SUCH AS YOUTUBE WILL FLAG IT AS A COPYRIGHT VIOLATION AND MAKE YOU TAKE IT DOWN.

FOLDERS

When you save your file—simple-sound.py—make sure that it is in the same folder as the sound you are using; in this case, with whirl.ogg.

The programs you've written until now only involve one file. But as your programs become more complex and you add sounds, images, and more functionality, it will be important to keep your files organized in folders. In order to keep everything tidy, it is good practice to create a new folder for each program you create.

When you call a file (such as the whirl.ogg file you just used) from within your Python program, Python will automatically check for the file in *the same* folder that your Python program is saved in. If the file you're trying to call is in a different folder, you will have to tell Python which folder to look in by changing the file directory. For example:

click_sound = pygame.mixer.Sound("/Users/elizabethtweedale/Python/sounds/whirl.ogg")

Now, the sound is inside a "sounds" folder.

```
import pygame                                           # import Pygame—load all of the pygame resources
pygame.init()                                           # initialize Pygame—setting it up
screen = pygame.display.set_mode([400, 400])            # set the screen size to 400 x 400 pixels—try changing these numbers and see how it updates
pygame.display.set_caption('Super Skills')              # set the caption of your screen to anything you like, ours is called 'Super Skills'
mouse_sound = pygame.mixer.Sound("whirl.ogg")           # label your sound and load in the file—you can call 'click_sound' anything you like
key_sound = pygame.mixer.Sound("blip.ogg")              # NEW LINE! Lable and load another sound for pressing any key
soundboard = True                                       # this is a boolean (True/False), which tells our program to continue—it can also be named anything
while soundboard:
    for event in pygame.event.get():                    # this is the main drawing event loop of the program—it captures any events that will happen
        if event.type == pygame.QUIT:                   # if the user quits the program, tell the program to stop
            soundboard = False
        elif event.type == pygame.MOUSEBUTTONDOWN:      # if the user clicks the mouse...
            mouse_sound.play()                          # play the sound loaded in
        elif event.type == pygame.KEYDOWN:              # NEW LINE! If the user presses any key
            key_sound.play()                            # NEW LINE! Play the sound loaded in for pressing any key
print ("Goodbye Soundboard!")                           # print to the IDLE screen when you exit
pygame.quit()                                           # quit Pygame
```

Remember to create a new folder for each project. Here we've named our folder "sounds." The "sounds" folder sits inside the "elizabethtweedale" folder—"elizabethtweedale" is the username of the author of this book. Your folder will have your own username in it!

IMAGES

Now add an image to your soundboard. Find images just like you did with sounds. You can either use the image we used from GitHub (https://github.com/elizabethtweedale/HowToCode2) or find your own from one of these websites:

www.pixabay.com or
www.pexels.com

In this example, you will write a program to play a sound if you click on the left-hand side of the image and to stop the sound if you click on the right-hand side of the image.

We are now using five modules from Pygame:

1. pygame.display: This handles how the **GUI** window will look in our program.

2. pygame.mixer: We use this to handle our sound functions.

3. pygame.image: This gives us all the image functionality we will need.

4. pygame.event: This tells us when events like moving and clicking happen in our program.

5. pygame.mouse: In this example, this tells us where the mouse is on the screen.

After typing any of these followed by a "." into the IDLE file, a list of suggestions pops up. These are the functions that are included in each of the modules.

```
import pygame

pygame.init()                                          # initialize Pygame—setting it up

screen = pygame.display.set_mode([800, 600])           # set the screen size to 800 x 600 pixels—it should be the same size as the picture!
pygame.display.set_caption('Super Skills')             # set the caption of the screen—this one is called "Super Skills"

click_sound = pygame.mixer.Sound("whirl.ogg")          # label the sound and load in the file—can call it "click_sound" for example

background_position = [0, 0]                            # set the position of the background to start in the top left corner, which is [0, 0]
background_image = pygame.image.load("lion.jpg").convert()   # label the image and load in the file—can call "background_image" for example

soundboard = True                                      # this is a boolean (True/False) which tells our program to continue

while soundboard:
    for event in pygame.event.get():                   # this is the main drawing event loop of the program, it captures any events that will happen
        if event.type == pygame.QUIT:                  # if the user quits the program, tell the program to stop
            soundboard = False
        elif event.type == pygame.MOUSEBUTTONDOWN:     # if the user clicks the mouse...
            player_position = pygame.mouse.get_pos()   # find the position of the mouse
            x = player_position[0]                     # return the "x" coordinate (left to right/horizontal axis)
                                                       # y = player_position[1]  # this is what we could use to return the "y" coordinate

            if x < 400:                                # if "x" is on the left half of the picture
                click_sound.play()                     # play the sound loaded in
                print ('Left Side Click', x)           # print the position to the console (just as a test - we don't actually need this line of code)
            else:
                click_sound.stop()                     # else if "x" is on the right half of the picture, stop the sound
                print ('Right Side Click', x)          # again, print the position as a test

    screen.blit(background_image, background_position)  # set the background image and tell it where its position is
    pygame.display.flip()                               # flip the screen to draw the background

pygame.quit()
```

YOU CAN FIND A LIST OF FUNCTIONS ONLINE IN THE PYTHON AND PYGAME DOCUMENTATION SECTIONS. THIS IS ALSO HANDY FOR LOOKING UP HOW TO CALL EACH FUNCTION, WHAT THEY TAKE AS INPUTS, AND WHAT INFORMATION THEY CAN RETURN TO YOU.

A MORE COMPLEX SOUNDBOARD

Now that you've made a basic soundboard that can play one sound if you click on a certain part of the screen, let's explore making a more complex soundboard that can play multiple sounds depending on where you click or which button you press.

For this program, you will need to download a few more sound files. You can also choose a new image such as a picture of a piano, a photo that has four different **coordinates,** or just an image that you like.

```
Python 3.5.2 (v3.5.2:4def2a2901a5, Jun 26 2016, 10:47:25)
[GCC 4.2.1 (Apple Inc. build 5666) (dot 3)] on darwin
Type "copyright", "credits" or "license()" for more information.
>>>
=== RESTART: /Users/elizabethtweedale/Documents/pygame-soundboard-lion.py ===
Left Side Click 178
Left Side Click 250
Right Side Click 622
Right Side Click 733
Right Side Click 446
Left Side Click 4
Right Side Click
>>>
=== RESTART: /Users/elizabethtweedale/Documents/pygame-art-soundboard-lion.py ===
Top Left Click 248    42
Top Right Click 692   112
Bottom Left Click 181   313
Bottom Right Click 617   353
Top Left Click 235    56
Top Right Click 609   70
Bottom Left Click 237   255
Bottom Right Click 773   381
Bottom Right Click 401   411
Top Left Click 175    68
Top Right Click 698   72
Bottom Right Click 737   369
Bottom Left Click 280   407
>>>
```

```python
import pygame
pygame.init()

screen = pygame.display.set_mode([800, 500])
pygame.display.set_caption('Super Skills Art Soundboard')

top_left_sound = pygame.mixer.Sound("whirl.ogg")
bottom_left_sound = pygame.mixer.Sound("blip.ogg")
top_right_sound = pygame.mixer.Sound("charm.ogg")
bottom_right_sound = pygame.mixer.Sound("sleep.ogg")

background_position = [0, 0]
background_image = pygame.image.load("art.jpg").convert()

soundboard_end = False

while not soundboard_end:
    for event in pygame.event.get():
        if event.type == pygame.QUIT:
            soundboard_end = True
        elif event.type == pygame.MOUSEBUTTONDOWN:
            player_position = pygame.mouse.get_pos()
            x = player_position[0]
            y = player_position[1]
            if x < 400:
                if y < 250:
                    top_left_sound.play()
                    print ('Top Left Click', x , y)
                else:
                    bottom_left_sound.play()
                    print ('Bottom Left Click', x , y)
            else:
                if y < 250:
                    top_right_sound.play()
                    print ('Top Right Click', x , y)
                else:
                    bottom_right_sound.play()
                    print ('Bottom Right Click', x , y)

    screen.blit(background_image, background_position)
    pygame.display.flip()

pygame.quit()
```

\# notice how this is the opposite of what we've done before

\# now we are saying while it is NOT the end...

\# and instead of changing True to False, we are changing False to True

\# this gives us the "x" position of the mouse click
\# this gives us the "y" position of the mouse click
\# left side
\# top
\# play the top left sound

\# bottom
\# play the bottom left sound

\# right side
\# top
\# play the top right sound

\# bottom
\# play the bottom right sound

BECOME A VIDEO GAME DESIGNER

There are two main things to master in order to create a video game: designing the game and programming the game. In this Super Skill, you'll learn a bit about both of these.

To start designing a game, consider these four elements.

1. **The player character**—Who is the player character and how does it move?

2. **The scene**—Where is the player character? Does the scene change?

3. **The goal**—What is the player character trying to do?

4. **Interactions**—What kind of things or characters interact with the player character? Are there enemies? Are there things the player character collects?

In the last Super Skill, you learned how to use Pygame to load images, react to a mouse event, and play sounds. You can now use this skill to start designing your first game.

1. **The player character**—a tiny robot that can move up, down, left, and right

2. **The scene**—a circuit board

3. **The goal**

   - Gold bugs appear on the circuit board in **random** locations.

   - The robot will try to collect as many gold bugs as it can in 60 seconds.

   - An enemy robot tries to catch the robot to stop it from stealing its gold bugs.

   - If the enemy robot catches the tiny robot, the game is over.

To get started, you will program a robot player that will move around the screen by pressing the arrow keys. Then you'll program the game to play a sound when the player character hits the edge of the screen.

Let's take a look at the structure of the code you'll be writing. It goes like this.

- At the beginning of the program, import any libraries you need.

- Next you write the **set up** code.

- Load files such as images and sound.

- Define any **variables** you will be using in the program.

- Finally, start the Pygame **"event" loop**.

Now let's take a look inside the "event" loop. There are three main sections to think about as you're organizing your code.

- **Event processing**—This keeps track of every event that happens during your game and what you should do when each event happens.

- **Game logic**—This will be where you write the rules of the game.

- **Drawing code**—This is where you draw all of the images and shapes.

- **Update clock**—This is telling the game clock to keep ticking.

- **Flip the display**—Writing the code is like drawing it on the reverse of a piece of paper. Flipping it over will show you the drawing!

PSEUDOCODE

The specific instructions a programmer writes are called **algorithms**. Using **pseudocode** is a useful way of writing an algorithm before you code it. It is written in any language, a bit like the way you would speak, but kept as close to the actual programming language as possible. For example, when writing pseudocode, it's helpful to use coding-style terms such as "if…then…else" and loops. It's also helpful to indent different parts of your pseudocode to help you see how the code will look when you move on to writing it. It's basically a mixture of how you would speak and how you would code, so it's a great way to plan out your program.

Here's how your program could look in pseudocode.

```
Import:
      pygame
Set up code:
      Set up pygame
      Set up Clock
            Set up the Screen & label it
Load files:
      Background Image
      Player Image   <------
      Sound

Set player position - x,y

Start Pygame loop:
      Event processing:
            If player quits, exit pygame loop
            If player pushes a key   <------
                  If LEFT key, move player left (subtract 20 from x)
                  If RIGHT key, move player right (add 20 to x)
                  If UP key, move player up (subtract 20 from y)
                  If DOWN key, move player down (add 20 to y)
      Game logic:
            If the player is at the edge of the screen,
                  then play sound.
      Drawing:
            Draw Background
            Draw Player   <------
      Update Clock
      Flip Display
If exited from Pygame loop, quit.
```

We will load an image for our player. You might have to resize your image to make it small enough to fit in your game. You can do this with a simple paint program.

We're changing the event listener to respond to specific keys instead of the mouse button.

It is important to pay attention to the order that these are in. Imagine each thing you draw to the screen as its own piece of paper. If you put the tiny robot player down first and then the background image, you wouldn't see the tiny robot!

Now that we've written the pseudocode, it will be much quicker to write the real code. Here it is:

```
import pygame

''' SET UP CODE HERE '''
pygame.init()                                          # set up Pygame
myClock = pygame.time.Clock()                          # start Clock

myScreen = pygame.display.set_mode([1000, 625])        # set up Screen
pygame.display.set_caption('Robot Bounce')             # set up Caption

myBackground = pygame.image.load('circuits.png').convert()   # load Background

myPlayer = pygame.image.load('robot.png').convert()    # load Player
myPlayer.set_colorkey((0,0,0))

mySound = pygame.mixer.Sound('laser.ogg')              # load Sound

playerX = 500                                          # set Player's X position
playerY = 300                                          # set Player's Y position

done = False                                           # main event loop:
while not done:
    ''' EVENT PROCESSING HERE '''
    for event in pygame.event.get():
        if event.type == pygame.QUIT:
            done = True
        elif event.type == pygame.KEYDOWN:
            if event.key == pygame.K_LEFT:
                playerX -= 20
            if event.key == pygame.K_RIGHT:
                playerX += 20
            if event.key == pygame.K_UP:
                playerY -= 20
            if event.key == pygame.K_DOWN:
                playerY += 20

    ''' GAME LOGIC HERE '''
            # if the player is at the edge of the screen, then play a sound
    if playerX <= 0 or playerX >= 1000 or playerY <= 0 or playerY >= 625:
        mySound.play()                                 # play Sound

    ''' DRAWING CODE HERE '''
    myScreen.blit(myBackground,[0,0])                  # draw Background
    myScreen.blit(myPlayer, [playerX-30, playerY-50])  # draw Player

    myClock.tick(60)                                   # tick Clock
    pygame.display.flip()                              # flip Display

pygame.quit()
```

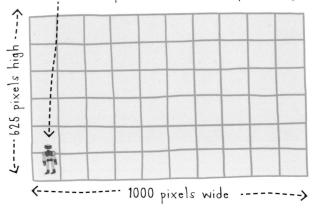

robot is 60 pixels wide and 90 pixels high

625 pixels high

1000 pixels wide

When Pygame places these images within the screen, it always starts at the top left corner. Which is why we write:

myScreen.blit(myBackground,[0,0])

In order to draw the player in the middle of the background image, we need to subtract half of the width and half of the height from the x and y coordinates.

myScreen.blit(myPlayer, [playerX-30, playerY-45])

COORDINATES AND PIXELS

Coordinates and **pixels** become even more important when designing games. It's helpful to draw things out with their measurements as you go along. For example: if your background image is 1000 x 625, draw a rectangle labeled 1000 wide and 625 high. If your player image is 60 x 90, draw a rectangle with the robot labeled 60 wide and 90 high.

ADDING MORE GAME ELEMENTS

Refer to the complete code on pages 56–57 to check where to insert your exciting game elements.

ADD GOLD BUGS

First draw an ellipse (to be your gold bug) at a **random** location on the screen. Then, when the player character reaches it, change the location of the bug so that it looks as though the player character has collected it.

The location of the bug will change each time the player character reaches it, so let's create a **function** to update the position to a new random location. The **newPosition( )** function will return a random (x,y) coordinate to use. Add it ABOVE your set up code because it is a new definition.

```python
def newPosition():                  # define a function to return a new (x,y) position
    randomX = randint(0,1000)       # find a random integer between the left and right edge
    randomY = randint(0,625)        # find a random integer between the top and bottom edge
    return (randomX, randomY)       # return the random x and y coordinates
```

To create the bug, add this in the set up code:

```python
myBug = newPosition()       # create new Bug Position
GOLD = (255,200,0)          # define GOLD Color
```

In the game logic, add:

```python
if playerX <= (myBug[0]+30) and playerX >= (myBug[0]-30):
    if playerY <= (myBug[1]+50) and playerY >= (myBug[1]-50):
    mySound.play()
    myBug = newPosition()
```

Instead of a picture, we can also use Pygame to draw shapes like we did with the Turtle library. This code draws an ellipse on the screen, with the color, the location (x position, y position), and the size you define (width, height).

In the drawing code, add:

```python
pygame.draw.ellipse(myScreen,GOLD,(myBug[0],myBug[1],10,20)
```

- -

ADD A SCORE

To add a score, you first need to create a **variable** called **score** and set it to start at 0. Then, each time the player character reaches a bug, you simply need to add one to the score. In the set up code, add:

In the game logic, inside the two "if" statements, add:

Score	00
Timer	00

```python
score = 0        # set Score to 0
```

```python
score += 1; print ('Score:',score)    # add 1 to
                                       # the score
```

ADD A TIMER

For a countdown timer, use the Pygame Timer. Create a new variable called Time and set it to start at 60 and count down each second.

In the set up code, add:

```
pygame.time.set_timer(pygame.USEREVENT, 1000)
time = 60          # set Time to 60 seconds
```

You can also update the code in the event processing:

```
elif event.type == pygame.KEYDOWN and time > 0:
    # time > 0 will ensure the timer doesn't run out
```

This will make it so the player can only move if the time is greater than zero.

And add this in the event processing as well:

```
elif event.type == pygame.USEREVENT:
    if time > 0:
        time -= 1    # time -= will subtract 1 from the time
                     every second until it reaches 0
```

WRITE TO THE SCREEN

It is helpful to write text on your game screen so that the player can see their score and the countdown timer. We call this **writing to the screen**.

To write to the screen, first set the type of font you want to use. Font is the style of the typeface, including its size, its weight (thickness), and the color of the characters.

In the set up code, add:

```
myFont = pygame.font.SysFont("monospace", 30)
```

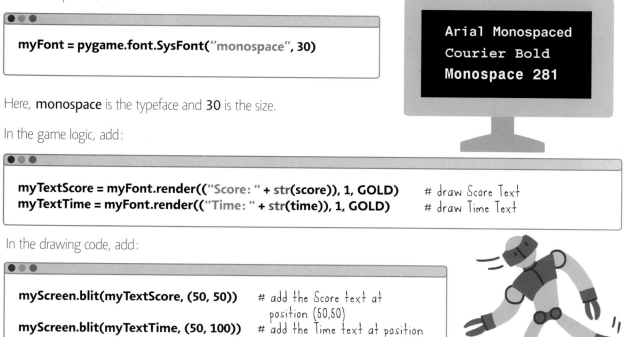

Here, **monospace** is the typeface and **30** is the size.

In the game logic, add:

```
myTextScore = myFont.render(("Score: " + str(score)), 1, GOLD)    # draw Score Text
myTextTime = myFont.render(("Time: " + str(time)), 1, GOLD)       # draw Time Text
```

In the drawing code, add:

```
myScreen.blit(myTextScore, (50, 50))     # add the Score text at
                                           position (50,50)
myScreen.blit(myTextTime, (50, 100))     # add the Time text at position
                                           (50,100) (which is 50 pixels
                                           below the Score)
```

ADD AN ENEMY

What's a game without an enemy? Add an enemy robot that is trying to catch your robot. If the enemy catches the player character, the game will be over. You can also add a special move to make the enemy jump to a new random location every 5 seconds. To start, add a new definition to make the enemy follow the player. We can even tell it how fast to move (in terms of the number of pixels it moves each time the screen updates).

```python
def followPlayer(e,p,s):          # e = enemy position, p = player position, s = speed
    x,y = e[0],e[1]
    if e[0] < p [0]:
        x = (e[0] + s)
    else: x = (e[0] - s)
    if e[1] < p [1]:
        y = (e[1] + s)
    else: y = (e[1] - s)
    return (x, y)
```

In the set up code, add:

```python
myEnemy = pygame.image.load('enemy.png')      # load Enemy
myEnemy.set_colorkey((0,0,0))
enemyPos = newPosition()                       # create New Enemy position
```

In the event processing, inside the "USEREVENT if" statement, add:

```python
if time%5 == 0:          # Move the enemy every 5 seconds
    enemyPos = newPosition()
```

In the game logic, add:

```python
# if the player position matches the enemy position, set time to 0 for GAME OVER
if playerX <= (enemyPos[0]+60) and playerX >= (enemyPos[0]-60):
    if playerY <= (enemyPos[1]+100) and playerY >= (enemyPos[1]-100):
                time = 0
# if time is not 0, the enemy follows the player
if time > 0:
    enemyPos = followPlayer(enemyPos,(playerX,playerY),3)
```

In the drawing code, add:

```
myScreen.blit(myEnemy, [enemyPos[0]-30, enemyPos[1]-50]) # draw Enemy
```

Finally, if time is 0, print "GAME OVER" to the screen. Add this to the bottom of the drawing code:

```
if time == 0:
    myScreen.blit(myFont.render("GAME OVER",1,GOLD), (50, 150))
```

Congratulations—you've made your first game! Here's the final code all together for you to check that you wrote it in the correct order. Now you can try changing the images, updating the logic, and using different variables to create a new game!

```
import pygame
from random import randint

def newPosition():                                    # define a function to create new random positions
    randomX = randint(10,990)                         # find a random integer between the left and right edge
    randomY = randint(10,615)                         # find a random integer between the top and bottom edge
    return (randomX, randomY)                         # return the x and y coordinates for the coin

def followPlayer(e,p,s):                              # e = enemy position, p = player position, s = speed *** NEW DEFINITION ***
    x,y = e[0],e[1]
    if e[0] < p [0]:
        x = (e[0] + s)
    else: x = (e[0] - s)
    if e[1] < p [1]:
        y = (e[1] + s)
    else: y = (e[1] - s)
    return (x, y)

''' SET UP CODE HERE '''
pygame.init()                                         # set up Pygame
myClock = pygame.time.Clock()                         # set up Clock
pygame.time.set_timer(pygame.USEREVENT, 1000)         # set up Timer

myScreen = pygame.display.set_mode([1000, 625])       # set up Screen
pygame.display.set_caption('Bug Collecting')          # set up Caption

myBackground = pygame.image.load('circuits.png').convert()   # load Background

myPlayer = pygame.image.load('robot.png').convert()   # load Player
myPlayer.set_colorkey((0,0,0))
myEnemy = pygame.image.load('enemy.png').convert()    # load Enemy            #** NEW LINE **#
myEnemy.set_colorkey((0,0,0))                                                 #** NEW LINE **#

mySound = pygame.mixer.Sound('laser.ogg')             # load Sound

myFont = pygame.font.SysFont("monospace", 30)         # load Font

myBug = newPosition()                                 # create New Bug position
enemyPos = newPosition()                              # create New Enemy position    #** NEW LINE **#

playerX = 500                                         # set Player's X position
playerY = 300                                         # set Player's Y position

score = 0                                             # set Score to 0
time = 60                                             # set Time to 60 seconds
GOLD = (255,200,0)                                    # define GOLD Color

done = False                                          # main event loop
while not done:
```

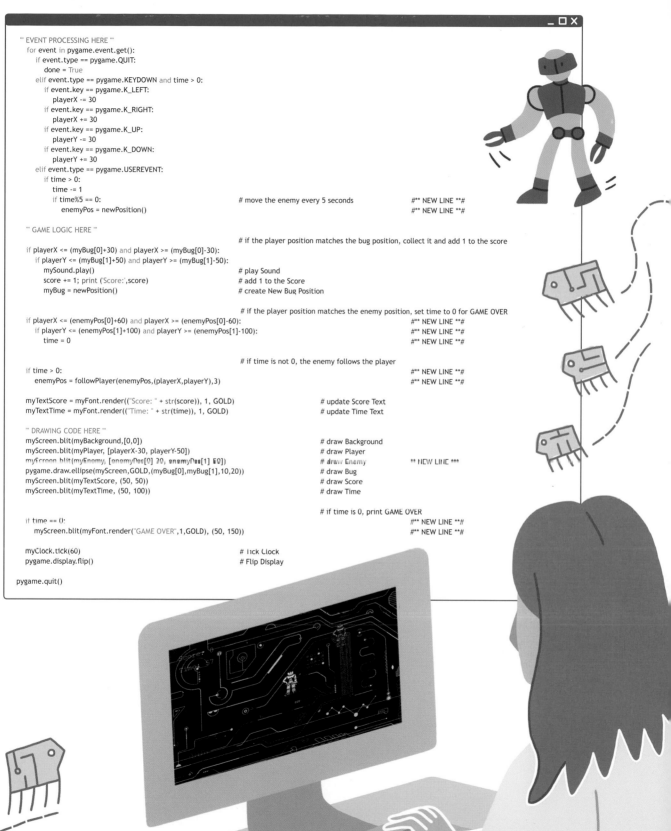

```
''' EVENT PROCESSING HERE '''
    for event in pygame.event.get():
        if event.type == pygame.QUIT:
            done = True
        elif event.type == pygame.KEYDOWN and time > 0:
            if event.key == pygame.K_LEFT:
                playerX -= 30
            if event.key == pygame.K_RIGHT:
                playerX += 30
            if event.key == pygame.K_UP:
                playerY -= 30
            if event.key == pygame.K_DOWN:
                playerY += 30
        elif event.type == pygame.USEREVENT:
            if time > 0:
                time -= 1
                if time%5 == 0:                         # move the enemy every 5 seconds          #** NEW LINE **#
                    enemyPos = newPosition()                                                      #** NEW LINE **#

''' GAME LOGIC HERE '''
                                                        # if the player position matches the bug position, collect it and add 1 to the score
    if playerX <= (myBug[0]+30) and playerX >= (myBug[0]-30):
        if playerY <= (myBug[1]+50) and playerY >= (myBug[1]-50):
            mySound.play()                              # play Sound
            score += 1; print ('Score:',score)          # add 1 to the Score
            myBug = newPosition()                       # create New Bug Position

                                                        # if the player position matches the enemy position, set time to 0 for GAME OVER
    if playerX <= (enemyPos[0]+60) and playerX >= (enemyPos[0]-60):                               #** NEW LINE **#
        if playerY <= (enemyPos[1]+100) and playerY >= (enemyPos[1]-100):                         #** NEW LINE **#
            time = 0                                                                              #** NEW LINE **#

                                                        # if time is not 0, the enemy follows the player
    if time > 0:                                                                                  #** NEW LINE **#
        enemyPos = followPlayer(enemyPos,(playerX,playerY),3)                                     #** NEW LINE **#

    myTextScore = myFont.render(("Score: " + str(score)), 1, GOLD)     # update Score Text
    myTextTime = myFont.render(("Time: " + str(time)), 1, GOLD)        # update Time Text

''' DRAWING CODE HERE '''
    myScreen.blit(myBackground,[0,0])                   # draw Background
    myScreen.blit(myPlayer, [playerX-30, playerY-50])   # draw Player
    myScreen.blit(myEnemy, [enemyPos[0]-30, enemyPos[1]-60])    # draw Enemy       ** NEW LINE ***
    pygame.draw.ellipse(myScreen,GOLD,(myBug[0],myBug[1],10,20))    # draw Bug
    myScreen.blit(myTextScore, (50, 50))               # draw Score
    myScreen.blit(myTextTime, (50, 100))               # draw Time

                                                        # if time is 0, print GAME OVER
    if time == 0:                                                                                 #** NEW LINE **#
        myScreen.blit(myFont.render("GAME OVER",1,GOLD), (50, 150))                               #** NEW LINE **#

    myClock.tick(60)                                    # Tick Clock
    pygame.display.flip()                               # Flip Display

pygame.quit()
```

BECOME AN APP DEVELOPER

For the final Super Skill, learn to become an app developer so that you can share the projects you've completed with others…particularly with those who cannot code in Python!

PACKAGING YOUR APP

"App" is short for "application." A computer application is a program that runs on your computer after being installed. Packaging it is a very important part of being an app developer and programmer. It is what we call **deploying** your code, which is how you will distribute your program to users. To do this, you will need to package up, or **compile**, your code using a library called PyInstaller. With this, you will be able to convert Python scripts into standalone applications.

PyInstaller allows you to make your program work on a computer, that doesn't have Python installed. It will place all of your code (and any dependencies such as the robot image in your game) into an executable file. The executable file can then be installed, opened, and run on someone else's computer as an app.

An important thing to note about PyInstaller when you're packaging your apps is that the **output** executable file you create will only work in the same environment that you are using to develop your code with. For example, if you are using a Mac, your app will automatically be a Mac app. If you are using Windows, your app will be Windows based, etc.

TAKE IT FURTHER

SINCE YOU CAN ONLY CREATE AN APP FOR THE ENVIRONMENT YOU'RE USING, WHY NOT TRY TO FIND A FRIEND WHO HAS A DIFFERENT OPERATING SYSTEM? YOU COULD USE THEIR COMPUTER TO PACKAGE YOUR APP IN A DIFFERENT ENVIRONMENT!

INSTALL PYINSTALLER

Let's install PyInstaller. The easiest way to do this is using **pip**, a package management system used to install and manage software packages written in Python. It automatically installs on your computer when you install Python.

○ On a Mac, you can simply open the Mac terminal and type:

```
pip3 pip install pyinstaller
```

○ On a Windows computer, you will use pip-Win. You can try searching for this in your applications if you haven't used it before.

When pip-Win is open, enter this command in its Command field and click Run:

```
venv -c -i pyi-env-name
```

The **pyi-env-name** can be anything you want, as long as it is one word, with no spaces. This creates a new virtual environment at C:\Python\pyi-env-name and makes it the current environment. A new command **shell** window opens in which you can run commands within this environment. Enter the command:

```
pip install PyInstaller
```

To use PyInstaller once it is installed:

○ Start pip-Win

○ In the Command field, enter venv pyi-env-name

○ Click Run

Then you have a command shell window in which commands, such as PyInstaller, can be run in a Python-style environment.

HANDY TIP!

If pip doesn't work for you or seems confusing, you can download and install PyInstaller, as you have done with previous libraries such as Pygame, by going to: www.pyinstaller.org. Take a look at the information and documentation on the website if you have questions.

HOW PYINSTALLER WORKS

These are the steps PyInstaller goes through so that you can deploy your app.

1. PyInstaller reads a Python script written by you.

2. It analyzes your code to discover every other **module** and library your script needs in order to execute.

3. It collects and copies all of those files, including the Python interpreter, and puts them with your script into a single folder with its dependencies.

4. It creates a single executable file with the same name as your Python script.

To run PyInstaller, you will do so from the terminal or **Command line**. Once you have this opened, for most of your programs, it is as simple as one short command:

```
pyinstaller myscript.py
```

There is an added option, such as a **windowed** (for Mac) or **onefile** (for Windows) application. This creates a single executable file, which is useful if you have images or sounds included. For example, on a Mac:

```
pyinstaller --windowed myscript.py
```

On Windows:

```
pyinstaller --onefile myscript.py
```

By default, PyInstaller will look for your Python script inside your main directory folder. You can either make sure your script is inside this folder or change the directory you are in before calling PyInstaller.

Try testing PyInstaller on one of your previous scripts, such as the sketch program.

For Mac:

```
pyinstaller --windowed sketch-program-2.py
```

For Windows:

```
pyinstaller --onefile sketch-program-2.pypy
```

You can test out the app yourself by running the executable file which was just created.

As a further test, try creating an app with your musician soundboard and your robot game! PyInstaller will include the Pygame resources needed for your soundboard game to run as well. It is important to note that some scripts will work better than others with PyInstaller. Packaging simple scripts such as the spy's cipher code or the teacher's bubble sort work really well, because they only include modules that are native to Python.

REMEMBER, THE OUTPUT OF PYINSTALLER IS SPECIFIC TO THE ACTIVE OPERATING SYSTEM AND THE ACTIVE VERSION OF PYTHON.

DISTRIBUTING YOUR APP

Once PyInstaller bundles your app, you will be left with one folder and one executable file. In order to deploy your program, all you need to do is compress the folder into a zip file. To do this, simply right-click on the folder and choose Compress (on a Mac) or Zip (in Windows) in the menu. Once you send the zipped folder to your users, they will install the program by simply unzipping it. The user can then run your app by opening the folder and launching the executable file inside it.

HANDY TIP!

If your executable file is not inside your app folder when it is created by PyInstaller, make sure to move it inside the folder before you zip it.

CONGRATULATIONS!

You have now learned ten Super Skills using Python! Along the way, you have tried out all kinds of different careers, such as becoming a programmer, an artist, a fashion designer, an architect, a spy, a teacher, a musician, a video game designer, and, finally, an app developer. Great job!

Whether you stick with Python or decide to try out other programming languages, you can use the skills you've learned in this book as you continue to explore. Even if you don't continue with computer programming, understanding the fundamental ideas of programming will help you at school and with all kinds of things throughout your life, such as your career. Have fun, stay curious, and never stop exploring technology and the world around you.

USEFUL LINKS

Congratulations! You have now mastered 10 Super Skills that make you a coder. Here are some resources you can use to learn more and build other great projects.

THE AUTHOR'S WEBSITE

www.cyphercoders.com

A good place to go if you'd like to find out more about learning to code!

GITHUB

https://github.com/elizabethtweedale/HowToCode2

Github is useful for storing and sharing your code. You can find all of the code from this book here.

PYTHON

www.python.org

The official Python website where you can download and find information about all things Python-related!

STACK OVERFLOW

www.stackoverflow.com

If your code isn't working, this is a good place to ask questions and get advice about text-based programming languages.

TOUCH TYPING

www.ratatype.com
www.typingclub.com

Free online websites for learning and practicing your touch typing skills.

OPEN SOURCE

www.opensource.org

A website where you can learn more about open source software.

PYGAME

www.pygame.org

Pygame is a cross-platform library designed to make it easy to write multimedia software, such as games, in Python.

FREE SOUNDS

www.opengameart.org
www.freesound.org

If you need sound clips for your programs you can download open source sound clips here.

FREE IMAGES

www.pixabay.com
www.pexels.com

Websites that have free images and videos for you to use in your projects.

PYINSTALLER

www.pyinstaller.org

Download PyInstaller to package your Python programs into stand-alone executable files.

GLOSSARY

ALGORITHM A set of specific instructions written as a procedure or formula for solving a problem. Computer programs are written with algorithms.

COMMAND LINE Programmers use the command line to communicate with the operating system of your computer.

COORDINATES A mapping of the position of pixels on the screen represented by two integers, the X-axis (left to right) and the Y-axis (top to bottom).

CPU The command center of the computer that communicates your instructions to and from the Input and Output Devices, the memory, and networks.

EVENT An event is something that happens while a program is running. For example, moving the mouse, clicking a button, or typing on a keyboard.

EVENT HANDLER The event handler receives information from the event loop about what kind of event has occurred. It then finds the relevant code telling the program what to do if that specific event happens.

EVENT LOOP An event loop is used by a program to continually check on what's happening and looks for events that the user might be giving to the computer.

FOR LOOP A loop used for repeating code a specific number of times.

FUNCTION A function is code included in Python, or written by you, that can be reused to perform different tasks.

GITHUB Github is a website used to store and share code.

GUI Graphical User Interface— pronounced "gooey." This is the screen you interact with when communicating with the computer.

IDLE Interactive Development Environment. It is a software you can use to write and run Python programs.

INPUTS All of the information that enters the computer such as key strokes and mouse movements.

INTEGER A whole number.

INTERPRETER The Python Interpreter helps you pick up on any bugs in your code. Its job is to translate what we are telling it into a language that the computer can understand!

MODULE A module is made up of code. It is like a library of books and each book is a module.

OPEN SOURCE SOFTWARE Software with source code that anyone can inspect, change, and improve.

OUTPUTS All of the information that comes out of a computer, such as the information on the screen or sound.

PARAMETER A parameter is like a variable that allows a programmer to pass information or instructions into functions and procedures within their program.

PIXEL The tiny points that make up a computer screen.

PSEUDOCODE A useful way of writing an algorithm before you code it.

RANDOM Something that is unexpected or not in an expected order.

TERMINAL Application used to send commands directly to the computer's operating system.

TKINTER Tkinter is Python's built-in GUI module.

VARIABLE Information in a program that can and is expected to change— such as the time, your mood, or the weather.

WHILE LOOP Also known as an infinite loop, repeats code UNTIL a specific objective is met.

INDEX